How Children Learn Language

Within three years of birth, children acquire several thousand words, figure out how to build and understand complex sentences, and master the sound system of their language – all before they can tie their shoes.

How do children learn language? How can they be so good and so fast – better even than the most gifted adult?

In this engaging and accessible book, William O'Grady provides a highly readable overview not only of the language acquisition process itself, but also of the ingenious experiments and techniques that researchers use to investigate this mysterious phenomenon. It is ideal for anyone – parent or student – who is curious about how language works and how it is learned.

WILLIAM O'GRADY is Professor of Linguistics at the University of Hawaii. His previous publications include *Syntactic Development* (1997) and *Syntactic Carpentry: An Emergentist Approach to Syntax* (2004).

Cambridge Approaches to Linguistics

General editor: Jean Aitchison, *Rupert Murdoch Professor of Language and Communication, University of Oxford*

In the past twenty-five years, linguistics – the systematic study of language – has expanded dramatically. Its findings are now of interest to psychologists, sociologists, philosophers, anthropologists, teachers, speech therapists, and numerous others who have realized that language is of crucial importance in their life and work. But when newcomers try to discover more about the subject, a major problem faces them – the technical and often narrow nature of much writing about linguistics.

Cambridge Approaches to Linguistics is an attempt to solve this problem by presenting current findings in a lucid and non-technical way. Its object is twofold. First, it hopes to outline the "state of play" in key areas of the subject, concentrating on what is happening now, rather than on surveying the past. Secondly, it aims to provide links between branches of linguistics that are traditionally separate.

The series will give readers an understanding of the multi-faceted nature of language, and its central position in human affairs, as well as equipping those who wish to find out more about linguistics with a basis from which to read some of the more technical literature in books and journals.

Also in the series

How Children Learn Language

WILLIAM O'GRADY
University of Hawaii

CAMBRIDGE
UNIVERSITY PRESS

PUBLISHED BY THE PRESS SYNDICATE OF THE UNIVERSITY OF CAMBRIDGE
The Pitt Building, Trumpington Street, Cambridge, United Kingdom

CAMBRIDGE UNIVERSITY PRESS
The Edinburgh Building, Cambridge, CB2 2RU, UK
40 West 20th Street, New York, NY 10011–4211, USA
477 Williamstown Road, Port Melbourne, VIC 3207, Australia
Ruiz de Alarcón 13, 28014 Madrid, Spain
Dock House, The Waterfront, Cape Town 8001, South Africa

http://www.cambridge.org

© William O'Grady 2005

First published 2005
Third printing 2006

Printed in the United Kingdom at the University Press, Cambridge

Typeface Photina 10/12 pt.   *System* LaTeX 2_ε [TB]

A catalogue record for this book is available from the British Library

Library of Congress Cataloguing in Publication data
O'Grady, William D. (William Delaney), 1952–
How children learn language / William O'Grady.
     p.   cm. – (Cambridge approaches to linguistics)
Includes bibliographical references and index.
ISBN 0 521 82494 X – ISBN 0 521 53192 6 (pbk.)
1. Language acquisition.   I. Title.   II. Series.
P118.0268   2004
401′.93 – dc22

ISBN 0 521 82494 X hardback
ISBN 0 521 53192 6 paperback

Contents

Acknowledgments

I am grateful for the assistance and insightful advice of several readers of earlier versions of this manuscript – Miho Choo, Woody Mott, Michiko Nakamura, Kevin Gregg, Kamil Deen, Ann Peters, Keira Ballantyne, Sunyoung Lee, Jung-Hwa Kim, Jin-Hee Kim, Jung Hee Kim, and Brendan and Leah O'Grady. I have also benefited from helpful comments by students in my classes at the University of Hawaii and in Professor Kyung-Ja Park's class at Korea University. In addition, I owe a debt of gratitude to two anonymous referees and to the superb editorial team at Cambridge University Press – Andrew Winnard, Helen Barton, Paul Watt, Anna-Marie Lovett, and Jacque French. Finally, I am especially grateful to Cathleen Marie O'Grady for her help collecting the artwork and preparing the index.

1 Small talk

Most of the time we adults take language for granted – unless of course we have to learn a new one. Then, things change pretty quickly. We can't get the pronunciation right, and we can't hear the difference between sounds. There are too many new words, and we forget ones that we learned just the day before. We can't say what we want to say, and we can't understand anything either, because everyone speaks too fast.

Then, as if that isn't bad enough, we come across a three-year-old child and watch in envy and amazement as she talks away effortlessly in that impossible language. She can't tie a knot, jump rope, draw a decent-looking circle, or eat without making a mess. But while she was still in diapers, she figured out what several thousand words mean, how they are pronounced, and how they can be put together to make sentences. (I know that I've used "she" all the way through this paragraph, as if only girls learn language. Since English doesn't have a word that means "he or she," I'll simply alternate between the two. I'll use "she" in this chapter, "he" in the next chapter, "she" in the third chapter, and so forth.)

Children's talent for language is strangely limited – they're good at learning language, but not so good at knowing what to say and what not to say.[1]

> "Daddy, did your hair slip?" – *three-year-old son, to his bald but long bearded father*
>
> "Why don't you get some expensive money?" – *three-year-old daughter, when told by her mother that she could get a small toy, but that the ones she had asked for were too expensive*
>
> "I wish someone we knew would die so we could leave them flowers." – *six-year-old girl, upon seeing flowers in a cemetery*
>
> "If I was a raccoon, I would eat the farmer's corpse." – *a kindergartener, writing a story about what he would do if he were a raccoon*
>
> "How will that help?" – *kindergarten student, when the class was instructed to hold up two fingers if any of them had to go to the bathroom*

These samples of "childspeak" are funny because of the misunderstandings that they contain about rather basic things in the world – beards, money, raccoons, death, going to the bathroom in kindergarten, and so on. It's easy to lose sight of what they *don't* contain – mispronunciations, words with the wrong meanings, or grammatical errors.

There is something very intriguing about this. Despite their naiveté about the world in general, children can make and hear contrasts among dozens of speech sounds, they have learned thousands of words without having heard a single definition, and they are able to build and understand sentences of impressive complexity. Herein lies the mystery of language acquisition. How can children be so good at language, and so bad at almost everything else?

Sounds, words, and sentences

From a parent's point of view, the most important and exciting thing about language acquisition is probably just that it allows their children to talk to them. But exactly what does it take to be able to talk? And how do children get from the point where they can't do it to the point where they can?

Most children start producing words some time between the ages of eight and twelve months or so, and many children have ten words in their vocabulary by the age of fifteen months. Things gradually pick up speed from that point on. Whereas an eighteen-month-old child may learn only one or two new words a day, a four-year-old will often acquire a dozen, and a seven-year-old will pick up as many as twenty. (That's more than one per waking hour!)

How does this happen? Adults don't pause between words when they speak, so how do children figure out where one word ends and another begins? How do they learn to make words plural by adding the suffix -*s* and to put verbs in the past tense by adding -*ed*? Why do we find errors like *eated* and *goed*? Why do children say things like *I can scissor it* and *I sharped them*?

By themselves, words are just empty shells, and there's no point in learning a new word if you can't also learn its meaning. Children are remarkably good at this too – so good in fact that they are often able to learn a word's meaning the first time they hear it used. For instance, a child who sees a horse running in a field and hears her mother say "horse" typically figures out right away that the word refers to the animal, not to its color, or to its legs, or to the fact that it's running. What makes this possible?

Meaningful words are the building blocks out of which we create sentences, our principal message carriers. Most children begin producing sentences some time between the ages of eighteen and twenty-four months, at about the point where they have vocabularies of fifty words or so. First come two-word utterances like (*Mommy here* and *That mine*), then longer telegram-like sentences that are missing little words like *the* and *is* as well as most endings (*That a green one. Mommy drop dish*).

By the age of three, the basics of sentence formation are in place and we find many sentences worthy of an adult – *I didn't know that one stands up that way*, *Does that one get a button?*, and so on.[2] How does a child master the craft of sentence carpentry at such an early point?

A whole different set of challenges face the child when it comes to the *meaning* of sentences. How, for example, is a child who can only say one or two words at a time able to make herself understood? How does she figure out that *The car was bumped by the truck* means the exact opposite of *The car bumped the truck* even though the words *car*, *bump*, and *truck* occur in the same order in both sentences? Why doesn't *The doll is easy to see* mean that the doll can see well?

And then there are speech sounds – the stuff of nightmares for adult language learners. Just how does a child go about distinguishing among dozens of speech sounds? And, equally importantly, how does she go about figuring out how to *make* those sounds and then assemble them into fluent melodies of syllables and words? What, if anything, does babbling have to do with all of this? Do children really produce all the sounds found in human language before learning to speak their own?

All of which brings us to the ultimate question: how DO children learn language? Every time I'm asked that question, my first inclination is to respond by simply saying that I wish I knew. In a way, that's the most honest answer that anyone can give. The fact of the matter is that we still don't understand how children learn language – any more than we have figured out how the universe works, exactly what happened to the dinosaurs, or why we can't all live for two hundred years.

But that doesn't mean that we are completely in the dark. On the contrary, research in the last three decades has yielded many exciting and important findings that reveal a great deal about how language is acquired. The job of this book is to report on those findings in a way that makes them accessible to scholars, students, and parents who are not specialists in the field of language acquisition research.

Methods 101

There are basically two ways to go about studying child language. The first is called "experimental," because it involves conducting experiments. Contrary to popular belief, experiments don't have to involve a laboratory or special equipment – although some do.

An experiment is really just a way to test an idea. Good experiments are often ingeniously simple, and you don't have to be a specialist to understand them. In the chapters that follow, we'll have a chance to look at the results of some of the most famous of these experiments to see what they tell us about children and their language.

The second way to study child language is called "naturalistic," since it relies on the observation of children's speech in ordinary everyday situations. Two techniques are particularly popular.

One involves keeping a language diary. For the first few months after a child begins to talk, it may be possible to write down each and every one of her utterances – or at least each and every one of her NEW utterances. (For those of you who'd like to keep your own diary, you'll find some guidelines in Appendix 1 at the end of the book.)

By the time a child is two years old, though, she typically becomes so talkative that it's impossible to keep up. From that point on, a diary is usually used just to make note of more specific sorts of things, like the pronoun in *My did it* or the double past tense in *I ranned away*. A different research technique is needed to keep track of other aspects of development.

As a child becomes more loquacious, acquisition researchers often gather naturalistic data by recording samples of her speech and conversations, usually for about an hour every two weeks. (These days, researchers like to make video recordings rather than just audio recordings. That allows them to have a record not only of what children say but also of what they are doing, what they are looking at, what gestures they use, and so on.) Once transcribed and analyzed, these speech samples become a linguistic "photo album" that captures many of the major milestones in a child's journey to language.

Thanks to the efforts of dozens of researchers over the past thirty years, there is now a significant database of child speech transcripts, both for English and to a lesser extent for various other languages as well. These are available to everyone through the Child Language Data Exchange System, or CHILDES (http://www.childes.psy.cmu.edu/).[3] (In case you'd like to do some recording and transcription of your own, I've included some basic information in Appendix 1.)

As we will see in the chapters that follow, both observational and experimental techniques have a place in the study of child language. Each is appropriate for answering particular types of questions, and each is subject to limitations that may make it inappropriate for other types of research. You'll see lots of examples of how both techniques are used as we proceed.

What's next

To make our task more manageable, it helps to divide language into its component parts – sounds, words, sentences, meanings, and so on – and deal with them in separate chapters. This is a bit of a distortion, I admit, since children don't first learn sounds, then words, then sentences, and then meanings.

In reality, children start using words and learning meanings before they master all of a language's sounds. And they usually start building sentences after they acquire just a few dozen words. So, there's actually an extended period of time during which children are working on sounds, words, meanings, and sentences all at once. But it'll be a lot easier for us to figure out what's going on if we can untangle these different things and look at them separately.

We'll get started on all of this in the next chapter by talking about how children identify and learn the words of their language. But if you're more interested in how they learn meanings, or sentences, or sounds, feel free to skip ahead to another chapter. Each chapter can be read independently of the others and, hopefully, each will pique your curiosity about what comes next.

Just one word of reassurance before beginning, especially for readers who have young children of their own at home. When it comes to language acquisition, all children share the same destination, but no two follow exactly the same path or travel at exactly the same speed. Except in the rarest of cases, these differences should be a cause of delight rather than concern. Children need people who will listen to them and talk to them. Beyond that, they typically do very well on their own, so there's no need to take on the role of teacher. Just watch and listen – something amazing is about to happen.

2 The great word hunt

A child's first birthday is cause for special celebration in most cultures. It's a sign of survival and growth. By this age, children have their first teeth, they are able to eat solid food, and they're about ready to take their first steps, if they haven't already done so.

Their minds are developing too – they are able to follow the direction of an adult's gaze, they are sensitive to gestures such as pointing, and they tend to pay attention to the same things as the adults with whom they are interacting.[1] Not coincidentally, this is also about the time that they first venture into language.

A child's first word is one of the great milestones in his life – and in the lives of his parents. For most children this happens when they are around twelve months old, give or take a few weeks in either direction. On average, a child has ten words in his vocabulary by age fifteen months and fifty words by age eighteen or nineteen months.[2]

And, yes, it's true that the first words learned by children the world over are usually the names for "mother" and "father." They get a lot of help with this, though. As we'll see in chapter 6, words like *mama*, *papa*, and *dada* are very easy to pronounce – they consist of very simple sounds arranged into very simple syllables – and they are a natural by-product of children's spontaneous babbling. In fact, "mama"-like sounds have been detected in children's vocalizations starting from as early as two weeks of age up to around five months, usually in a "wanting" context (wanting to be picked up, wanting food, and so on).[3]

Parents are quick to help a child assign meaning to these early noises, decreeing that *mama* means "mother" and *papa* or *dada* means "father." Children go along with the game, it seems, and before long they start using those words in just the "right" way. (The game is played differently in Georgian, a language spoken in one of the former Soviet republics in the Caucasus Mountains. There, I'm told, *mama* means "father"!)

At first, word learning is quite slow and new words show up at the rate of one every week or so. But things often speed up at about the time children reach the fifty-word milestone (usually around age eighteen months). At this point, we often see the beginnings of a "vocabulary spurt" during which children learn one or two new words a day.[4]

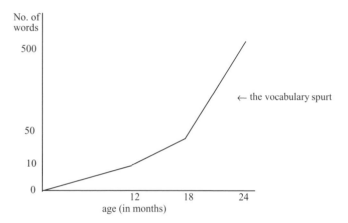

In some children, the spurt doesn't take place until the vocabulary contains well over one hundred words.[5] And as many as a third of all children acquire words at a steady pace or in a series of small bursts with no sudden leap forward.[6] (It's even been suggested that the whole idea of a vocabulary spurt is a myth,[7] although most linguists still seem to believe in it.)

At later ages, word learning becomes even faster, averaging about ten words a day between age two and six.[8] By age six, children have a vocabulary of about 14,000 words,[9] and they go on to learn as many as twenty new words per day over the next several years.[10] (Try to do that day in and day out if you're learning a foreign language.) The average high school graduate knows 60,000 words.[11]

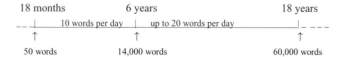

1. Where are the words?

You may not realize it, but when people talk, they usually don't leave pauses between their words. Most sentences are just a single continuous stream of sounds. If you have any doubts about this, try listening to a language that you don't speak. You'll quickly notice that the words all run together.

That should give you some idea of the challenge that a child confronts as he tries to learn English. Somehow, he has to take the continuous stream of sounds that make up a sentence like *Wewatchedthedoggiesrun* and break it down into words (like *doggies* and *run*) and pieces of words (like the past tense ending *-ed* and the plural ending *-s*). Linguists refer to this process as *segmentation*.

Sometimes we make things easy for children by producing utterances that consist of just one word – like when we point to something and say "Milk" or when we pick up a spoonful of food and say "Open." But we don't do that as often as you might think – one-word sentences like these make up only about 10 to 20 percent of parents' speech to children.[12]

Children forge ahead anyway, picking what they can out of the stream of speech that flows past their ears. The things they grab onto are often single words, but sometimes they end up with larger bites of speech – like *what's that?* (pronounced *whadat*) or *give me* (pronounced *gimme*).

These are almost certainly indivisible chunks for one-year-olds – the equivalent of the phrases that travelers commit to memory so that they can get by in a foreign country. (How many tourists who memorize *Arrivederci* as the Italian way to say "good bye" realize that it contains five separate meaning-bearing elements and literally means "until reseeing you"?)

A simple test helps us decide whether a particular utterance should be thought of as a multi-word sentence or an indivisible chunk with no internal parts: if there are multiple words and the child knows it, they should show up elsewhere in his speech – either on their own or in other combinations. That's what happens in adult speech, where the three words in *What's that?* can each be used in other sentences as well.

What's that?

What are they?   Get **that**.

The mail**'s** here.

But things don't always work that way in child language. Often, the different parts of an utterance behave as if they were welded together, with no hint that they have an independent existence of their own.

Other indications that an utterance is chunk-like come from the way it is used. For instance, two-year-old Adam often said "Sit my knee" when he wanted to sit on an adult's knee and "I carry you" when he wanted to be carried.[13] Both utterances were clearly modeled on things that he had heard adults saying to HIM, and he didn't seem to realize what the component parts were or what they meant.

A different type of segmentation error can be seen in the following utterances, which were produced by Adam when he was between twenty-eight and thirty-six months old.[14]

It's fell.
It's has wheels.
There it's goes.

These errors tell us that Adam must have misanalyzed *it's* when he heard it in sentences like *It's Daddy* and *It's hot.* Adults know that *it's* consists of the word *it* and part of another word (*is*), but Adam must have thought that it was a single one-part word. As a result, he started using *it's* where an adult would use *it* – as we can see in his *it's fell* and *it's has wheels.*

Two learning styles

Some children are initially better than others at finding words. In fact, there appear to be two different styles of language learning.[15]

The *analytic* style focuses on breaking speech into its smallest component parts from the very beginning. Children who use this style produce short, clearly articulated, one-word utterances in the early stages of language learning. They like to name people (*Daddy*, *Mommy*) and objects (*kitty*, *car*), and they use simple words like *up*, *hot*, and *hungry* to describe how they feel and what they want.

However, other children take quite a different approach. They memorize and produce relatively large chunks of speech (often poorly articulated) that correspond to entire sequences of words in the adult language.

Child's utterance	Meaning
Whasdat?	"What's that?"
dunno	"I don't know"
donwanna	"I don't want to"
gimmedat	"Give me that"
awgone	"All gone"
lookadat	"Look at that"

This is called the *gestalt* style of language learning. ("Gestalt" is the German word for shape. It's used by psychologists to refer to patterns that are perceived as wholes.)

It is probably best to think of the analytic–gestalt contrast as a continuum. No child employs a completely analytic strategy or a purely gestalt style. Rather, children exhibit tendencies in one direction or another.

Is there a reason why some children are more toward the gestalt end of the continuum and others more toward the analytic end? Perhaps. We'll come back to this question in the next chapter when we talk about the meanings of children's early utterances. For now the important thing is simply this: both approaches to language learning work equally well, so there's no reason to be concerned about whether a particular child is following the right path. He is.

2. How children find words

Children are incredibly good at breaking jumbles of speech sounds into smaller, more manageable units. In one experiment, eight-month-old infants listened to two minutes of speech consisting entirely of random combinations of syllables that were run together the way they are written below:[16]

dapikutiladotupirogolabu . . . dapikutupirotiladogolabu . . .
tupirodapikutiladogolabu

At the end of the two-minute period, the experimenters played some made-up three-syllable "words" for the infants. Some of these "words" were new, but some – like *tupiro* – had been in the original passage (yes, it's in there three times!).

Amazingly, the children were more likely to turn their head in response to items that had been in the passage than to ones that hadn't. Since head-turning in infants is a sign of noticing, we know that they somehow were able to recognize the syllable combinations that were in the two minutes of gibberish that they had been listening to.

What types of clues and strategies do children use to break up real sentences into smaller units, like words, prefixes, and suffixes? Fortunately for children, words have a fairly regular profile in the sound pattern of a language, and it gets easier to recognize that profile the more you encounter it.

One of the most reliable features of a word's profile in English involves stress – the tendency for some syllables to be more audible than others. Say the following sentence aloud and see if you can identify the stressed syllables.

The bird might land on the fence.

Here's what you probably noticed – there's a stressed syllable in *bird*, *land*, and *fence*, but not in the other words.

The BIRD might LAND on the FENCE.

This simple example actually reflects a very reliable tendency in English. Nouns and verbs tend to have stress on at least one of their syllables while other types of words (like *the*, *might*, and *on*) generally do not.

Spotlights

Ann Peters and Svend Strömqvist have suggested a vivid metaphor to describe what may be going on here – stress is like a "spotlight" that draws a child's attention to particular syllables, making them easier to pick out.[17]

The Spotlight Strategy
Pay attention to stressed syllables.

Other work suggests that the spotlight seeks out more than just stressed syllables – it also seeks out certain stress *patterns*.

A very frequent stress pattern in English nouns consists of a stressed syllable followed by an unstressed syllable (the so-called "strong–weak" pattern that poets call a "trochaic foot") – BAby, DOCtor, CANdle, DOGgie, and so on. (English also contains weak–strong patterns, such as giRAFFE, guiTAR, and adVICE, but these are less frequent.)

Work by the late Peter Jusczyk and his colleagues has shown that children latch onto the strong–weak pattern at a very early age: infants who are just nine months old will listen longer to lists of words that have this stress pattern than to lists of words that don't.[18] (Infants who are listening to something turn their head toward it, so it's easy to determine when they lose interest and stop listening.)

Another series of experiments by Jusczyk and his colleagues presented seven-and-a-half-month-old children with a much more difficult task.[19] First, the children listened for forty-five seconds to passages that contained particular strong–weak words such as HAMlet.

> Your hamlet lies just over the hill. Far away from here near the sea is an old hamlet. People from the hamlet like to fish. Another hamlet is in the country. People from that hamlet really like to farm. They grow so much that theirs is a very big hamlet.

Then they listened to recorded lists of repeated words, some of which had occurred in the passage (*hamlet . . . hamlet . . . hamlet*) and some of which hadn't (*kingdom . . . kingdom . . . kingdom*).

Measurements of how long children turned their heads toward the loudspeaker revealed that they listened significantly longer to words that had appeared in the previous passage than to words that hadn't. This is very striking, especially since it is highly unlikely that seven month olds had any prior familiarity with words such as *hamlet*.

Can we be sure that it was actually the strong–weak pattern that the children were spotlighting? Could they perhaps have just been attracted to the stressed syllable in these words? We know that this wasn't happening, because the children showed no preference for the word *ham* after listening to the "hamlet story" – they were attracted only to the word *hamlet* itself.

Do children perhaps react positively to *any* two-syllable word, regardless of its stress pattern? No. Children didn't show a preference for words like *guiTAR*, which have a weak–strong stress pattern, when such items occurred in the initial passage.

> The man put away his old guitar. Your guitar is in the studio. That red guitar is brand new. The pink guitar is mine. Give the girl the plain guitar. Her guitar is too fancy.

Evidently, the children's spotlight is focused very precisely on the strong–weak stress pattern.

Another spotlight falls on combinations of consonants that are most likely to signal a break between words. Generally, for instance, the sequence "ng-t" occurs at a word boundary in English (as in *wrong time*) rather than inside a word. In contrast, the sequence "ng-k" occurs far more frequently inside words (as in *tinker* – the letter "n" represents an "ng" sound here).

In a remarkable experiment, nine-month-old infants listened to two lists of nonsense words. One list consisted of items containing consonant combinations that are most likely to occur *between* words (*nong-tuth*, for instance); the other list consisted of items containing consonant combinations that are most likely to be found *inside* words (*nong-kuth*, for example).[20]

List 1 (the *ng-t* combination – most likely *between* words)	*List 2* (the *ng-k* combination – most likely *inside* words)
nong tuth	nong kuth
chong tudge	chong kudge
poing tuv	poing kuv
zeng tuth	zeng kuth
vung tudge	vung kudge
goong tuv	goong kuv

When the items were pronounced with the strong–weak stress pattern typical of English two-syllable words, the children listened longer to the second list (with consonant combinations more frequently found inside single words).

However, when a half-second pause was inserted between the syllables, the children showed a preference for the first list (with consonant combinations that are typically found at word boundaries).

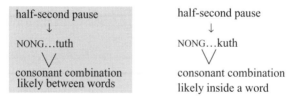

Evidently, the infants had come to associate consonant combinations such as "ng-t" with boundaries between words. And they had come to associate combinations such as "ng-k" with syllable boundaries within a single word. All before they had produced an actual word themselves!

Yet another spotlight seems to zero in on the ends of utterances. Experiments with children who've barely reached their second birthday show that they are more likely to respond correctly to the request "Find the dog," in which *the dog* occurs at the end of the sentence, than to "Find the dog for me," in which it occurs in the sentence's interior.[21]

There's even evidence that parents are at least subconsciously aware of children's sensitivity to this position. In a storytelling experiment, mothers placed unfamiliar words and words carrying new information at the ends of sentences 75 percent of the time – compared to 53 percent of the time when they were speaking to adults.[22]

Making matches

As children's vocabulary grows, another powerful word-learning tool known as the "Matching Strategy" comes into play.[23]

The Matching Strategy
When an utterance contains a part that matches something you already know, the matching part is a word and what's left over is too.

To see how this works, let's say that a child has already learned the word *doggie* and that he then hears his mother say *bigdoggie*. (I deliberately didn't leave a space here, because that's the way it must seem to the child when he first hears it; remember that speakers don't pause between words.)

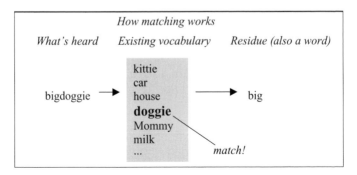

How matching works

What's heard	Existing vocabulary	Residue (also a word)
bigdoggie →	kittie car house **doggie** Mommy milk ...	→ big

match!

Thanks to the match between the last part of *bigdoggie* and the word *doggie* that he has already learned, the child knows not only that *doggie* is a word but also that *big* is as well.

One piece of evidence that things really work this way comes from children's comments and questions about language. The following remarks were made by Damon between the ages of two and three.[24]

> Windshield! Wind goes on it. That's why it's called a windshield.
> Eggnog comes from egg!
> You know why this is a HIGH-chair? Because it is high.
> A lady-bug. That like "lady".
> Does corn flakes have corn in it?
> Eve, you know what you do on runways? You run on them because they start with "run".
> [in a Safeway grocery store]: Is this where you get safe? 'Cause this is Safeway and you get safe from the cold.
> Do you know what headlights are? They're lights that go on in your head!

Damon's stream-of-consciousness comments reveal the Matching Strategy at work, as he suddenly recognizes the *wind* in *windshield*, the *egg* in *eggnog*, and the *high* in *highchair*. True, some of his matches are a bit off the target (headlights aren't lights that go on in your head), but even the mistakes confirm that matching is an important part of the segmentation process.

On occasion, the Matching Strategy may result in oversegmentation, leading a child to "find" a word where there isn't one. A well-known example of this involves the verb *behave*.

Because the *be* of *behave* sounds just like the *be* of *be good*, it triggers a match in some children when they hear their mother say "I want you to behave while I'm away." They mistakenly conclude that *have* (pronounced "hayve") must be a word too, which in turn leads them to say "I'm hayve" to mean "I'm good."[25] The road to segmentation is paved with good intentions.

Similar errors have been observed with "s" sounds that are misinterpreted as the plural marker -*s* because they occur at the end of a noun. Around age two, April was heard to say *bok* as the singular of *box*, *clo* as the singular of *clothes*, and even *sentent* as the singular of *sentence*.[26]

Misanalysis of word-final "s" in the speech of April

Word	April's "singular" form
box	bok
lens	len
trapeze	trappy
clothes	clo
Santa Claus	Santa Clau
sentence	sentent
upstairs	upstair

In general, breaking sentences into parts gets easier as children learn more words and become better at figuring out where one word ends and another one begins. However, even older children can make mistakes. A high school teacher, Amsel Greene, published a collection of word analysis errors made by her students.[27] One of her best examples came from a term paper:

In 1957 Eugene O'Neill won a Pullet Surprise.

Read the sentence aloud and you'll see what the student was trying to say: Eugene O'Neill won a Pulitzer Prize.

Identifying words is just the first step a child takes toward building a mental dictionary for his language. He also has to figure out what those words mean (that's discussed in the next chapter) and how they should be pronounced (we'll talk about this in chapter 6). In addition, he needs to know how to change words to make them plural or put them in the past tense. And he has to be able to create new words, so that he can talk about new things and situations. We'll look at these things next.

3. Learning inflection

English uses *inflection* (changes in the form of a word) to carry important bits of information. Two very obvious examples of this involve number and tense – plurality is expressed in English by adding the suffix *-s* to a noun, and the past tense is expressed by adding *-ed* to a verb. (We'll talk about irregular verbs shortly.) A lot can be inferred about how children learn language by investigating how they go about acquiring these two simple suffixes.

The plural ending -s

How can we know that a child has figured out that English has a general rule for forming plurals that involves adding the suffix *-s* to a noun? Just hearing him say a word like *dogs* to refer to more than one dog is not enough. He might just think that *dogs* is like *people* – an inherently plural word. Or he might think that the *-s* suffix is used to mark plurals on just a few words (like *-en* on *oxen*). Or he might just be remembering particular words that he has heard – without realizing that there is a general rule.

In a famous study conducted in the 1950s, Jean Berko figured out a simple way to find out what is really going on. She devised an experiment in which children had to pluralize made-up words as well as real words.[28] If children can pluralize words that they have never heard before, Berko reasoned, it must be because they have a general rule that adds the *-s* ending.

Here's how the experiment worked. Children were first shown a picture of a funny little creature and told "This is a wug." Then they were shown a picture of two of these creatures and the experimenter said:[29] "Now there is another one. There are two of them. There are two . . ."

THIS IS A WUG.

NOW THERE IS ANOTHER ONE.
THERE ARE TWO OF THEM.
THERE ARE TWO_____.

The "*wug* test," as it came to be called, was done with two groups of children – a group of preschoolers (aged four and five) and a group of first graders (aged five and a half to seven).

As you can see from the results in the following table, even the preschoolers did very well on the made-up words above the dotted line. They even knew when to pronounce the -*s* ending as "s" (for *heaf*) and when to pronounce it as "z" (all the other cases).

Percentage of correct responses on the
"wug" *test*

Nonsense word	Preschoolers	First-graders
wug	76%	97%
heaf	79	80
lun	68	92
tor	73	90
cra	58	86
tass	28	39
gutch	28	38
kash	25	36
nizz	14	33

Surprisingly, though, both groups of children did poorly on the words beneath the dotted line, for which they tended to simply repeat the singular form. Why did this happen?

If you listen carefully to the plural forms of the words in the second group, you'll notice something very interesting. The plural ending in these cases is not simply -*s*; it's -*es* – with the "e" pronounced as a weak vowel, rather like a "short i" sound.

Only words whose pronunciation ends in a "s," "z," "ch," "j," or "sh" sound form their plural this way. All other words use just -*s* (pronounced "s" or "z") as their plural ending, setting aside exceptions like *children* and *men*.

Words that take the -es ending	Words that take the plain -s ending
glass	cat
buzz	dog
lunch	back
judge	map
ash	finger

Children aged seven and under seem to know when to use the *-es* ending with *familiar* words – when asked for the plural of *glass*, they responded with *glasses*. But in contrast to the basic *-s* ending, they seemed not to have a general rule for *-es* that they can extend to *new* cases. This is a wonderful example of how even a simple experiment can reveal an important finding.

The past tense ending -ed

Although most English verbs form the past tense by adding the suffix *-ed*, there are several dozen "irregular" verbs that form their past tense in other ways – *eat/ate*, *go/went*, *sleep/slept*, *run/ran*, *come/came*, and *stand/stood* are obvious examples. Anyone who has been around a preschool child has almost certainly heard him say things like *eated*, *goed*, *sleeped*, *runned*, and *comed*. Evidently, irregular verbs present something of a problem.

A common scenario for the acquisition of an irregular verb like *go* looks something like this.[30]

> STEP 1: children use the "bare" verb *go*, with no tense marking at all. (e.g., Daddy GO to work.)
> STEP 2: they make sporadic use of the form *went*. (e.g., Daddy WENT to work/Daddy GO to work.)
> STEP 3: they begin to produce the "over-regularized" form *goed*. (e.g., Daddy GOED to work.)
> STEP 4: after some time (perhaps many months) *goed* gradually disappears in favor of *went*. (e.g., Daddy WENT to work.)

This is a classic example of what psychologists call "U-shaped" learning. That's because a line describing children's success over time resembles a U – it starts high (because of the initial correct use of a few irregular forms), then dips down to reflect the overuse of the *-ed* ending, and finally rises up again as children learn the exceptions to the general rule.

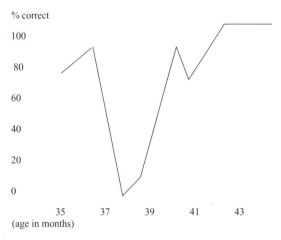

U-shaped development of the correct past tense for irregular verbs[31]

Recently, however, linguists have begun to think that this picture might not be entirely accurate.

Irregular verbs

In 1992, a group of researchers led by Gary Marcus published the results of a very detailed study of the past tense in child speech.[32] To the surprise of almost everyone, they found that children apparently don't use incorrect past tense forms all that often. In fact, on average, children aged two to five make mistakes with irregular verbs only 10 percent of the time. Moreover, none of the more than eighty children in the study produced incorrect past tense forms more than 25 percent of the time. There were even occasions when children seemed to know that they had made a mistake.[33]

Adult: Where's Mommy?
Child: Mommy goed to the store.
Adult: Mommy goed to the store?
Child: NO! (annoyed) Daddy, I say it that way, not you.
Adult: Mommy *wented* to the store?
Child: NO!
Adult: Mommy went to the store.
Child: That's right, Mommy wennn . . . Mommy goed to the store.

Marcus and his colleagues took their findings to mean that children learn the right past tense forms for most verbs – regular and irregular – very quickly. That is, they know from an early age that the past tense for regular verbs is formed by adding -*ed*; thus, *walk* becomes *walked*, *jump* becomes *jumped*, and so on. And they know that they have to set aside the general rule and retrieve a special form from their mental dictionaries for irregular verbs (e.g., *ran* for *run* and *ate* for *eat*).

Two ways to form past tenses

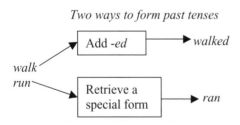

Problems arise when children who are just learning to talk take a wrong turn and end up on the more commonly traveled regular-verb path when they should be on the irregular-verb path. The result is an over-regularized form like *runned*.

Taking a wrong turn

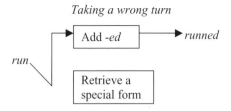

Sometimes, children even take both paths – first digging out an irregular form and then adding *-ed* to it. The result is a form like *wented* or *ranned*.

Following both paths

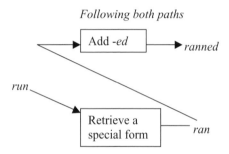

And, sometimes, they come up with the wrong irregular past tense form – like *writ* instead of *wrote* or *swang* instead of *swung*. Such errors may well reflect the influence of other irregular verbs – *write/writ* could be based on *bite/bit*, for instance, and *swing/swang* works just like *ring/rang*.[34]

In general, though, these types of errors are rare. And so are errors that involve treating a regular verb as if it were irregular – saying *wope* rather than *wiped* as the past of *wipe*, for example. A study of 20,000 verb forms in the speech of nine children revealed that less than two-tenths of 1 percent involve mistakes like *writ*, *swang* and *wope*.[35]

Irregular nouns

What about irregular nouns that form their plural with something other than just the *-s* suffix – nouns like *child/children*, *foot/feet*, and *wolf/wolves?* Children do sometimes produce plurals such as *childs* for *children*, *foots* for *feet*, and *wolfs* for *wolves*, but the error rate on irregular plurals is very low. In one study of preschool children ranging in age from fifteen months to five years, it was less than 10 percent, which is almost identical to the rate for irregular past tenses.[36]

This is a very intriguing finding. Irregular nouns are not very common in English; in fact, they make up less than 5 percent of the nouns children hear. In contrast, irregular verbs make up more than half of the verbs children hear. That's because there are far more irregular verbs than nouns, and many of the most common verbs in English are irregular.

If anything, then, we'd expect irregular plural forms to be swamped by the far more frequent -*s* suffix. But the proportion of "wrong turns" that children make with irregular plurals is about the same as it is for irregular past tenses. Evidently, here too children know what they are supposed to do, even if they occasionally fail to do it.

How many times do you have to hear me say that?

The finding that slip-ups in the expression of the past tense and the plural don't occur very often was surprising to many researchers. Most adults, including parents, have the impression that three- and four-year-old children produce incorrect past tense forms for irregular verbs pretty well all the time.

The truth may well lie somewhere in the middle – according to recent research by psychologist Michael Maratsos, overuse of the -*ed* ending is far more common with some irregular verbs than with others.[37] In particular, it seems that children are indeed relatively quick at figuring out the right past tense form for frequently heard irregular verbs like *go* and *see*, but that they may take much longer to master less common verbs such as *sink* or *win*.

Just how many times does a child have to hear an irregular verb before getting it right? Maratsos estimates that it may take several hundred exposures to the correct form before all over-regularizations are eliminated. This can happen quickly for frequently heard verbs, giving the impression that the learning of irregular forms is effortless. However, a somewhat different picture emerges for less frequent verbs, where high error rates can last for months as the child gradually accumulates enough experience to resist the temptation to over-regularize.

4. Creating words

A language's vocabulary is a work in progress. Words fall out of use (like *flytme*, an Old English word for a blood-letting instrument) and new words like *Internet*, *blog*, and *e-business* are added almost on a daily basis. (The latest edition of the *Oxford English Dictionary* added almost six thousand new items.)

Where do new words come from? Mostly from old words that are taken and refashioned in various ways – sometimes by giving them a new meaning, but often by giving them a new form as well. Children figure this out very quickly, and we need to understand it as well, if we are to keep up with them.

Three ways to create words

There are three especially popular strategies for creating a new word from an old word that we should look at before going any further.

1. Conversion

The simplest way to create a new word is to take a word that already exists and start to use it in a new way. Linguists call this process *conversion*, because it involves converting a word of one type into a word of another type.

Think of nouns and verbs, for example. I can take a thing-denoting noun like *canoe* and make it into an action-denoting verb with the meaning "travel by canoe" (*We canoed down the river*). And I can go in the other direction too – the verb *throw* can be turned into a noun (as in baseball, when you say *That was a great throw*).

Some nouns that have been converted into verbs	Some verbs that have been converted into nouns
BUTTER the bread	get a HIT
SHIP the package	give a KISS
INK a contract	feel the BITE
NAIL the door shut	want a HUG
BUTTON the shirt	get a RAISE

It's also possible to turn adjectives into verbs in English. For instance, I can take a property-denoting adjective like *dirty* and turn it into an action-denoting verb.

Conversion of "dirty," *the adjective, into* "dirty," *the verb*

dirty (adjective)	→	*dirty* (verb)
The floor is DIRTY. "not clean"		The workers DIRTIED the floor. "make dirty"

2. Derivation

A second major strategy for creating new words in English involves adding an ending to an already existing word to derive a new word with a new type of meaning. (Linguists call this *derivation*.) One of the most common endings of this type in English is *-er*, which attaches to a verb and creates a noun with the meaning "person who does x" or "thing used to do x."

Some examples of derivation with -er

teacher	a person who teaches
runner	a person who runs
sharpener	a thing used for sharpening
freezer	a thing used to freeze food

3. Compounding

A third very popular way to form new words in English involves *compounding* – putting together two or more already existing words. There are tens of thousands of compounds in English – *mailbox*, *blackboard*, *spaceship*, and *White House* are familiar examples.

Some compounds

streetlight	bluebird	swearword
campsite	happy hour	wash cloth
bookcase	highchair	crybaby

Some compounds are written with a space between their component parts and some without, so you can't rely on the way a word is written to know whether it's a compound versus a simple phrase.

A more reliable clue comes from the stress pattern: in a compound, the word to the left normally carries heavier stress than the word to the right – we say MAILbox not mailBOX. That's also why we say HOT dog for the thing that we eat, but hot DOG for an overheated canine. (The first one is a compound, and the second one is a simple phrase.)

Children don't just learn words. They create their own, including many that are not found in adult speech. Detailed diary records for one child revealed that he produced 1,351 different innovative nouns over a four-year period beginning when he was twenty months old – that's nearly one a day.[38]

Some innovations involve the overuse of conversion – like *to gun* for "shoot," or *to bell* for "ring." (The nouns *gun* and *bell* are converted to verbs when they shouldn't be.) Others, like *brakers* for "car brakes" and *cooker* for a "cook," involve the overapplication of a derivational suffix. Still others reflect an overeagerness to form a new compound – *sky-car* for "airplane" and *fix-man* for "mechanics," for instance.[39]

As we'll see next, these are more than just cute errors – they are valuable clues that can be used in conjunction with experiments to figure out how children go about building words. This deserves a more careful look.

I want to scissor it – learning conversion

Children start using conversion to create new words by the time they are two years old. Sometimes, though, they get ahead of the language and come up with words that they later have to "unlearn." Most conversion errors in English reflect the production of illegal verbs from nouns, especially from nouns that refer to objects that can be used as instruments or tools.

Some innovative verbs formed from nouns at ages two and three[40]

Example	Situation
And did you NEEDLE this? (= mend with a needle)	talking to his mother about a sock
But I didn't BLADE myself (= cut myself with the blade)	picking up a Cuisinart blade from the sink
How do you know where to SCISSOR it? (= open with scissors)	while trying to open a carton of apple juice
How do you WRENCH them? (= undo with a wrench)	unpacking a construction toy
An' WATER the dirt off my stick (= wash off with water)	talking about a hose in the garden
Not very wide, because it will WIND (= the wind will blow)	as his mother opened the car window
Will it WAVE in? (= come in via waves)	while digging a hole at the beach and discussing whether there will be water at the bottom

Some illegal verbs are formed from adjectives – as in *I'm talling* for "I'm growing tall" or *I'm still soring* for "I'm still feeling sore." Here are some other examples.

Some innovative verbs formed from adjectives at ages two and three[41]

Example	Situation
I SHARPED them (= sharpen)	speaking of two pencils
Are they SILLING? (= being silly)	children playing and laughing
I TIGHTED my badge and you should	speaking of a badge on his
UNTIGHT it (= tighten and loosen)	shirt

Children's overuse of conversion tells us something about what they find easy in language. They seem to like what Eve Clark has called "simplicity of form"[42] – they like to create words from other words without having to change them.

Simplicity of Form
Create new words from old words without changing their form.

The errors children make in applying this strategy are a good sign. Lots of English verbs ARE created from nouns. Maybe we don't needle things, but we do sometimes hammer them. And maybe we don't water dirt off sticks, but we do water lawns. Adults sometimes even create verbs from adjectives. They may not say *tight the badge*, but they do say *dirty the floor* and *clear the room*.

A child who says *Did you needle this?* or *I sharped them* has started to figure this out. He's gained a first foothold on the slippery slope of word formation.

It's crowdy in here – learning derivation

The study of children's early use of derivation reveals yet another preference in their word creation – they favor endings that are used on a large number of words. (Linguists call this *productivity*.)[43]

Productivity
Create new words from endings that can be used with many different words.

The first four derivational endings learned by Damon fit well with this strategy, since they were all among the most frequently used in English.

Endings in the speech of Damon prior to age four[44]

Ending	Meaning	Example
-er*	"doer"	walk**er**
-ie	"diminutive"	dogg**ie**
-ing	"activity"	Runn**ing** is fun.
-ness	"state"	big**ness**

*-er can also have an "instrument" meaning (as in *cutter* "something used for cutting"), but this is less frequent in children's early speech

We can also see the productivity strategy at work by comparing the endings -er and -ist.

Whereas -er can attach to almost any verb to give a noun with the meaning "one who does x" (*walker*, *runner*, *jumper*, *singer*, *eater*, and so on), -ist is very restricted in its use – we say *typist* but not *writist* (compare with *writer*), we say *cyclist* but not *skatist* (compare with *skater*), and so on. So we expect -er to be acquired early – and this seems to be exactly what happens, as the results of an experiment by Eve Clark and Barbara Hecht help show.[45]

Seated at a table with an experimenter, children aged three to six were given a chance to make up names for "doers" and instruments of various sorts.

For doers:
"I've got a picture here of someone who crushes things. What could we call someone who crushes things? Someone who crushes things is called a . . ."

For instruments:
"I've got a picture here of something that cuts things. What could we call something that cuts things? Something that cuts things is called a . . ."

Children of all ages liked to use -er in these situations. So, they tended to call someone who crushes things a "crusher" and something that cuts things a "cutter."

Sometimes, though, even a derivational ending can be overused. Take for example -y, which is very widely employed in English to turn nouns into adjectives – as in *salty*, *hairy*, and *furry*.

$$salt + y \rightarrow salty$$
$$\uparrow \qquad\qquad \uparrow$$
$$noun \qquad adjective$$

As the following examples help show, this process is sometimes over-exploited by young children.

Some innovative adjectives created by Damon at age two and three[46]

Example	Situation
It makes me WINDY (= blown by the wind)	as the car trunk was closed, creating a draft of air
At Anamaria's I saw a CRACKY hole (= a hole in a crack)	after seeing a picture of a manhole
The paper is SOAKY (= soaking wet)	referring to a wet newspaper
There's a ROCKY house (= made of rocks)	looking at stone walls in a ghost town
It's very NIGHTY (= pitch dark)	driving home in the dark
But not WALKY ones (ones that people can walk along)	talking about cliffs
It's a bit CROWDY in here (= crowded)	going into a parking lot
There's a BALLOONY store (= covered in balloons)	seeing a shop with balloons painted on the window
No, it's not POISONY (= poisonous)	talking about a flower

The *-er* ending too is sometimes overused by children, as when they call a cook a "cooker" or refer to a saw as a "sawer." (My six-year-old daughter liked to refer to her hair ties as "tiers.") For some reason, adult English chooses conversion over derivation to create nouns in these cases.

There's another type of mistake that children also make with *-er* words. Because *-er* is so commonly used to turn verbs into nouns, children seem to think that any noun ending in *-er* must have come from a verb. That's probably why many diary studies report sightings of the mysterious verb *hamm* in the speech of preschool children[47] – as in "We're gonna hafta hamm this nail."

Children's ability to make use of derivation to produce and understand new words develops slowly at first but grows from grades one to five. As the following fifth-grader demonstrated, a familiarity with derivation can be very useful indeed.[48]

EXPERIMENTER: What does the word *unbribable* mean?

CHILD: Never heard of that word . . .

EXPERIMENTER: OK. Do you think you might be able to use it in a sentence to show me you know what it means?

CHILD: The boy was unbribable.

EXPERIMENTER: OK. When you say "the boy was unbribable," what do you mean by the word *unbribable*?

CHILD: That you can't bribe him with anything.

EXPERIMENTER: And when you say you can't bribe him with anything, what does it mean to bribe?

CHILD: Um . . . sort of like talking him into something by using things.

EXPERIMENTER: OK. Can you give me an example?

CHILD: Um . . . I might talk you into giving me a phone number by giving you a piece of gum.

Skills like these remain useful throughout life. Remember that the next time you come across a word like *antidisestablishmentarianism*.

Let's go by sky-car – learning compounds

Children love compounds. In fact, about 80 percent of the innovative nouns heard in the speech of two- and three-year-olds are compounds, and the vast majority of these – including *sky-car* for "airplane" – are of the noun-noun type.[49] Here are some examples from children aged eighteen months to three years.

Child's word	intended meaning[50]
crow-bird	"crow"
car-smoke	"exhaust"
cup-egg	"boiled egg"
firetruck-man	"firefighter"
plant-man	"gardener"
store-man	"clerk"

Children also seem to have a very good idea of when it is appropriate to use a compound. In a naming experiment, children aged two to four were asked to make up names for objects in pictures – such as a house made out of pumpkin and a pan with a frog in it.[51]

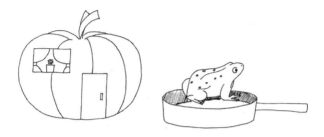

Even the youngest children were more likely to use a compound when there was an inherent connection between the two nouns than when the connection was only temporary or accidental. So, they were quick to describe the picture on the left as a "pumpkin house." However, they were much less likely to describe the picture on the right as a "frog pan," presumably because they think that the frog is only temporarily in the pan. This is exactly the type of contrast that we adults make in our use of compounds too.

Children's eagerness to use compounds hints at another of their preferences when it comes to creating words. In addition to simplicity of form, children also appear to like what Eve Clark calls "transparency of meaning" – they like building words whose meaning comes from the meaning of their parts.[52]

Transparency of Meaning
Create new words whose meaning comes from the meaning of their parts.

If you already know the word *store* and the word *man*, then it makes sense to create the compound *storeman* – especially if you haven't yet heard the word *clerk*.

But there are rules for forming compounds in English and it seems that children don't always follow those rules. Eve Clark and two of her colleagues collected some very interesting information on this from an experiment in which children aged three to seven had to make up names for people doing various types of things.[53] The experimenter would sit down with the child and show him a picture like the one below.

The dialogue would then go like this:

> "This is a picture of a boy who rips paper.
> What could we call him?
> A boy who rips paper is a . . ."

The children exhibited a clear preference for compounds – overall 69 percent of their responses were compounds like *paper ripper*. (When adults are asked, around 90 percent of their responses are compounds.) The next most common word-creating strategy among the children was to make up a non-compound word ending in *-er* (such as *ripper*). This strategy was used 23 percent of the time, on average.

What made the results really interesting, though, was that the children produced more TYPES of compounds than adults do. According to Clark and her colleagues, children go through three steps as they learn to create compounds that refer to "doers."[54]

- Step 1: Combine a verb with a noun like *man* that can refer to the doer (*wash-man*).

Compound type	Example	Intended meaning
verb + *man*	wash-man	someone who washes things
	open-man	someone who opens things

- Step 2: Combine a verb with a noun referring to the thing that is acted upon. In some of these patterns the verb is converted into a noun by a suffix such as *-er*.

Compound type	Example	Intended meaning
verb + noun	hug-kid	someone who hugs kids
	break-bottle	someone or something that breaks bottles
verb-*er* + noun	cutter-grass	someone who cuts grass
	giver-present	someone who gives presents
verb-*ing* + noun	washing-people	someone who washes people

The key feature of these patterns is that the words occur in the same order as in sentences. For example, we say "I cut the grass," with *cut* before *grass*, and this is also the order used in the child's compound *cutter-grass*.

- Step 3: Use of the noun + verb-*er* pattern preferred by adults.[55]

Compound type	Example	Intended meaning
noun + verb-*er*	wall builder	someone who builds walls
	house painter	someone who paints houses

Compounds and stress

Remember that one of the defining features of English compounds is stress on the first item – that's how we distinguish the hot dog that we eat from an overheated canine. But just how audible is this clue, and how useful is it to children?

An experiment involving children aged five to eleven and adults yielded a somewhat surprising result.[56] When asked to point to the picture of a *HOT dog* (versus a *hot DOG*), even adults were able to respond correctly only about three-quarters of the time. And children couldn't do that well until they were eleven years old – the younger children gave the right answer only about 55 to 60 percent of the time.

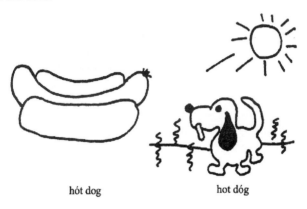

hót dog   hot dóg

The children's early strategy was simple. If the expression they heard resembled a familiar item, they interpreted it as a compound regardless of where the stress fell. So *hot dog* was always taken to refer to a sausage in a bun.

On the other hand, if the expression was unfamiliar, the children interpreted it literally. So the expression *red head* (which most parents said their children didn't know) was taken to mean a head that is red, not someone with red hair, regardless of where the stress fell.

Compounds and plurals

Compounds have another very interesting property that only shows up when you try to add a plural ending. Let's say that you hire three people to come by on Saturday morning and wash your car for you. What would you call them? Probably *carwashers*, which is just a compound (consisting of the smaller words *car* and *washer*) with a plural marker on the end.

car + washer + s

So far, so good. But now let's imagine that you have two cars and that you hire ONE person to wash both of them for you. What could you call that person? Well, you could call him a *carwasher*, but you couldn't call him a *carswasher* – even though he washes more than one car. That's because plural markers generally aren't allowed to occur inside compounds in English.

car + s + washer
    ↑
  plural marker inside compound

(One exception involves words like *clothes* and *scissors* that don't have a singular form; they are allowed to occur inside a compound – as in *clothesdryer*.)

When do children figure this out? From the very beginning, apparently. Peter Gordon devised an ingenious study to demonstrate this.[57] He made up a game in which children (aged three to five) had to make up compounds to describe different types of people. For example, he'd ask a child what to call someone who eats rice (a "rice eater") and what to call someone who builds a house (a "house builder").

The crucial items in the experiment contained plural nouns, as when the children were asked what they would call someone who caught rat**s**. Would they say "rat**s** catcher" (wrong) or "rat catcher" (right)? The children gave the correct answer 161 times out of 164 – a success rate of 98.1 percent!

Summing up

Children are great word finders and word makers. They are able to fish word-sized chunks out of the speech stream and they are able to figure out how to make words of their own. They know what they like (simplicity in form, transparency in meaning, and productivity) and they don't hesitate to play with the tools for word-making like conversion, derivation, and compounding.

Children's innovative words – *to needle* for "to mend with a needle," *nighty* for "dark as night," *hamm* for "hit with a hammer," and *sky-car* for "airplane" – leave no doubt as to what they are up to. More importantly, they give us a once-in-their-lifetime opportunity to witness the discovery of language.

We're not through with words yet. We've focused in this chapter on how words are discovered and built. But a word would just be an empty shell if it didn't have a meaning. Just how children figure this out is what the next chapter is all about.

3 What's the meaning of this?

As we saw in the previous chapter, children learn words at a breath-taking pace. By the time they enter school, they've learned the meanings of more than ten thousand words. Over the next several years, they will learn up to twenty more every day.[1] How does this happen?

Most of what we know about the acquisition of meaning involves nouns, especially words that denote objects (*dog*, *house*, *apple*, and so on). So, we'll start there, and focus on that in the first half of this chapter. The second half of the chapter looks at the sorts of meanings associated with other classes of words, including verbs, adjectives, and pronouns.

1. First meanings

Children are extraordinarily good at finding meanings for words – and words for meanings. In fact, they seem to be "primed" for this task before they even learn to speak, perhaps because words and their meanings help them organize and categorize the bewildering world that surrounds them.

In one experiment, a group of nine-month-old infants were shown a series of rabbit pictures as the experimenter said "a rabbit" each time. Another group saw the same pictures, but heard a tone instead. Both groups were then shown two pictures, one of a rabbit and one of a pig.

The group that had heard the "rabbit" label looked longer at the new animal. The group that had heard the tone made no distinction.

Evidently, hearing a label had helped the first group of infants recognize the category "rabbit," making it easier to see the pig as a new type of animal.[2]

Children have a very reasonable word-learning priority: they want to know the names for the people and things they've been seeing since they were born. So their first words tend to have meanings that are very close to home. To see this for yourself, look at the following list of words produced by a young boy over an eight-month period beginning when he was eleven months old. There are forty-three words in this list, and thirty-one of them are nouns – the type of word best suited for naming people and objects.

Tad's early words[3]

Age (months)	Nouns	Other
11	dog	
12	duck	
13	Daddy	yuk
	Mama	
	teh (teddy bear)	
	car	
14	dipe (diaper)	
	owl	
	toot toot (horn)	
15	keys	
	cheese	
16	eye	
18	cow	hot
	cup	
	truck	
19	kitty	happy, oops, pee pee
	juice	down, boo
	bottle	up, hi
	spoon	bye
	bowl	uh oh
	towel	
	apple	
	teeth	
	cheek	

(cont.)

Age (months)	Nouns	Other
	knee	
	elbow	
	map	
	ball	
	block	
	bus	
	jeep	

Among the non-nouns likely to show up in any child's "first fifty" list are words to comment on disappearance and absence (*gone*, *allgone*), the success or failure of an action (*there!*, *did-it*, *uh-oh*, *oh dear*), denial or rejection (*no*), calls for attention (*there*, *look*), vertical motion (*up*, *down*), and containment or attachment (*in*, *out*, *on*, *off*).[4]

Why nouns?

Why the early preference for nouns? One possibility has to do with the way parents talk to children. Although mothers use more verbs than nouns, they are more likely to prompt children to produce nouns (via questions such as "What's this?") than verbs.[5]

In addition, there is evidence that the nouns mothers use when they speak to children have meanings that might be easier to learn than those of the verbs they use. Whereas nouns tend to name solid objects with a similar shape (*cup*, *crayon*, and so on), verbs tend to be more diverse and variable. Some denote physical motion (e.g., *fall*) while others denote internal states (e.g., *want*). Moreover, some of the actions referred to by verbs involve a single entity (*go*), some involve two (*push*), and some involve three (*give*).[6]

1		1		2	1		2	3
Mary	went.	Mary	pushed	the car.	Mary	gave	a book	to a friend.

Another possible explanation for children's early attraction to nouns is that their perceptual system is specially attuned to noticing objects, particularly objects that satisfy the four conditions outlined below.[7] (Objects of this sort are sometimes called "Spelke objects" in honor of the researcher who first observed the importance of these conditions.)

Cohesion – Preferred objects consist of a connected and bounded region of matter. A ball is a good example of an object, since if you throw it, the whole thing will move as a single independent unit. A head, on the other hand, is not a good example of an object, since it is attached to something else.

Continuity – Preferred objects don't disappear at one point and reappear at another. Babies are surprised when one object passes behind another and then reappears on the other side. They evidently expect objects to have a continuous presence.

Solidity – Preferred objects don't pass through one another. Babies are surprised when they watch a film in which one object goes through another; they expect objects to be solid and impermeable.

Contact – Unless they are animate, preferred objects don't move without being touched. Experiments with babies reveal that they show surprise if an inanimate object (but not a person) moves on its own.

Noun-lovers and noun-leavers

All children seem to have more nouns than any other type of word in their early vocabulary, but the strength of the preference can vary from child to child. Children whose early vocabulary consists almost exclusively of nouns are sometimes called "referential" (the term "noun-lovers" has also been suggested), because so many of their early words are used to refer to people and objects. These children also tend to be more analytic, in the sense that they are good at breaking adult sentences down into word-sized pieces. (We talked about this learning style in the preceding chapter.)

Children who are less enamored with nouns are sometimes called "expressive" (or even "noun-leavers"!), since they tend to concentrate more on words and phrases that express relations and activities (e.g., *no*, *more*, *bye-bye*, *hi*, *let's go*, and so forth). They are also more likely to adopt a gestalt style of learning, so many of their first utterances are extra-sized chunks of speech whose component parts have probably not yet been identified (*whasdat*, *lookadat*, *gimmedat*, and so on).

Why are some children more referential and analytic while others are more expressive and holistic? It is sometimes suggested that these two learning styles reflect cognitive differences that can last well into the school years.[8]

One idea is that referential children are "patterners" who like to exploit the possibilities of the object world. When, for example, they play with toys, they enjoy using them to make patterns and structures.

In contrast, children whose early vocabulary is dominated by relational terms, by greetings, and by words for expressing feelings are more taken with the social world. Dubbed "dramatists," they prefer to focus on human interaction in their early play. Give patterners a tea set, it is said, and they'll use it to build a tower. Give dramatists a tea set, and they'll have a party.

The evidence for this hypothesis is mixed, though, and there is at least one other hypothesis that looks just as promising – namely that children's early vocabulary preferences reflect the way their parents interact with them linguistically.

Referential children tend to have mothers who like to draw their attention to object names and to indulge in the "What's that?" game. In contrast, mothers of expressive children tend to use more social formulae (*hi*, *bye*, *please*, *thank you*, *let's go*, and so on) when talking to them.[9] Although this doesn't rule out the existence of deep-seated (and perhaps inherited) differences in cognitive style, it raises the possibility that contrasts in vocabulary development are due simply to children's early experience with language.

2. Not enough and too much

Sometimes, children seem to have overly broad meanings for their words, and may therefore use them to refer to more things than the language allows. For example, *dog* might be used to refer to horses, cows, and other four-legged animals, in addition to canines. Such errors are called *overextensions*.

There's also such a thing as an *underextension* – having a meaning that is too narrow. A child might know the word *animal*, for example, but not realize that its meaning should include turtles and lizards as well as mammals.

Overextension of *dog*   Underextension of *animal*

turtles, lizards

It's even possible for the meaning of a single word to be both overextended and underextended at the same time. Quite often, for instance, children think that *alive* means "able to move by itself." This works quite well when it comes to people and animals. However, it also leads to problems, since children end up thinking that rivers and clouds are alive (an overextension), but that plants and trees aren't (an underextension).[10]

Over- and underextension of *alive*

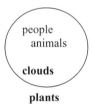

Underextensions are less often noticed than overextensions. This may be because they are simply less frequent. Or it may be because they are just harder to spot – someone who hears a child say "car" for the family automobile may not know that she never uses that word for anything else. Overextensions, on the other hand, are much more obvious – a child who points to a horse and says "dog" is going to be noticed!

If it looks like a duck . . .

Overextensions don't last very long, and most children stop using them altogether by age two or two and a half.[11] Nonetheless, they are quite common in the early stages of language learning. As many as 30 percent of the words used by one- and two-year-old children may have their meaning overextended at least some of the time.[12] (Indeed, one parental diary revealed an overextension rate for nouns of 40 percent in the speech of a one-year-old child.)[13]

As the examples below illustrate, overextensions are based primarily on perceptual similarity – the objects for which the word *quack* is used all look alike in some way (e.g., they all have wings, they are all small, and so forth).[14]

Some overextensions[15]

Word	First referent	Subsequent extensions
quack	duck	all birds and insects, flies, coins (with an eagle on the face)
tick tock	watch	clocks, gas-meter, fire hose on a spool, scale with round dial
fly	fly	specks of dirt, dust, small insects, child's toes, crumbs of bread
candy	candy	cherries, anything sweet
apple	apples	balls, tomatoes, cherries, onions, biscuits
turtle	turtles	fish, seals
cookie	cookies	crackers, any dessert
kitty	cats	rabbits, any small furry animal
box	boxes	elevators
belt	belts	watch strap
moon	moon	half grapefruit, lemon slice, dial on a dishwasher, vegetables in a picture, a crescent-shaped piece of paper

Although the similarities underlying extensions of a word's meaning usually involve movement, shape, size, sound, taste, or texture,[16] function can be important too.

If four-year-old children are told that one of the backward-L objects in the following picture is a "fendle," they normally assume that the other similarly shaped object (but not the S-shaped object)

is a fendle as well. However, if they see the larger object being used
as a container for the smaller one of the same shape, they are no
longer so eager to call it a fendle – apparently because they see that
it has a different function.[17]

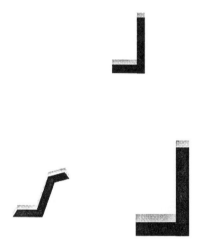

Sometimes both perceptual similarity and functional similarity play a role in a single series of overextensions. One child
overextended the word *clock* to watches, meters, dials, and timers of
various sorts – all of which have faces like clocks (a perceptual similarity). He then extended it to three new objects – bracelets, which
are worn on the wrist like a watch (a functional similarity), and
then a radio and a telephone, both of which have dials (a perceptual
similarity again).[18]

The path of overextension for "clock"

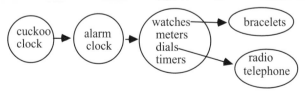

Did you do that on purpose?

A curious fact about all of this is that children don't usually overextend words that they have just learned. Rather, they tend to use a new word correctly for a few weeks before any overextensions appear.[19] This raises an interesting possibility.

Could it be that at least some overextensions are not real mistakes at all, but rather clever attempts by children to get the most mileage they can out of their limited early vocabulary? Is it possible that when they call a horse a dog, they're thinking "I know that's not really a dog, but I don't have a word for it or I can't remember it, so I'll have to use the closest thing I've got"?

One piece of evidence that overextensions may be deliberate comes from what happens when children learn the right word for the objects that they had been mislabeling. For example, two-year-old Allen was using the word *dog* for dogs, cats, sheep, and other four-legged mammals. But as soon as he learned the word *cat*, he stopped using *dog* for that type of animal, and as soon as he learned *sheep*, he no longer referred to those animals as dogs either.[20]

If Allen thought that *dog* meant "animal," learning the word *cat* wouldn't have changed anything. He could still have sometimes called felines dogs, just as you and I sometimes refer to them as animals. But that's not what he did; instead, he immediately stopped using the word *dog* for cats. That suggests that he probably never thought it meant "animal." He had just been "borrowing" it until the right word came along.

There's an even more direct way to figure out whether children know the meaning of words that they overextend. If children have the right meaning for a word in their head, they should understand the word correctly when someone else uses it. And this seems to be exactly what happens.

In one experiment, five children (twenty-one to twenty-five months old) who were overextending words were first given a naming task in which they were shown pictures and asked to name them.[21] Overextensions were identified and then used to design a comprehension test. For example, if the child overextended *dog* on the naming test to include cows, horses, cats, or sheep, the comprehension test would include pictures of these animals as well as a picture of a dog. The child would then be asked, "Show me the dog."

The results were quite dramatic. Overextensions in comprehension were much less frequent than in naming.[22] Moreover, when pictures of people were used, names such as *Daddy* that had been overextended in speech elicited no errors at all.

The tendency for overextensions to disappear in comprehension has been confirmed by larger-scale studies, including a high-tech experiment involving ninety-nine children.[23]

As illustrated below, the children sat between two TV monitors, each displaying a picture of a different animal – a dog and a pig, say. They then heard a word – *dog*, for instance. A device tracked their eye movement, recording which TV monitor they looked at and for how long.

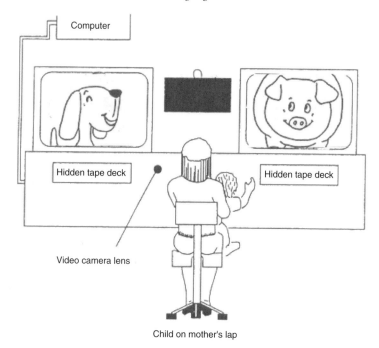

Child on mother's lap

More often than not, the children looked first and longer at the screen that matched the word they had just heard.

There's one possible exception to all of this, though. Two-year-old children do seem to overextend in comprehension at about the same rate as in production (around 30 percent) when they are dealing with less familiar concepts. So, although they rarely overextend a familiar noun such as *pig* in comprehension, they do make mistakes with less common nouns such as *hippo*, especially in situations where they are asked to choose among unfamiliar animals.[24]

3. Fast mapping

Overextensions notwithstanding, children are remarkably good at learning meanings. They have to be – otherwise they wouldn't be able to learn a new word every couple of hours or so, month after month. In fact, in a lot of cases, it seems that children are able to learn a new word after hearing it used only once or twice. Rapid learning like this is sometimes called *fast mapping.*

Fast mapping doesn't just happen with word meanings. It happens with facts in general. Children are just as quick at learning new facts about objects – that it costs a lot of money, it is used to mash potatoes, and so on.

Three- and four-year-olds who are shown a new object and told that it was "given to me by my uncle" are as good at remembering that fact a week later and a month later as they are at remembering that it is called a "koba." (Adults do well on both sorts of tasks too, suggesting that fast mapping is not just a child's sport.)[25]

A variety of experimental studies have documented just how good children are at fast mapping in the case of word meaning. In one experiment, children were taught new words as part of a helping game.[26] The experimenter would say things like "Oh, there's something that you could do to help me. Do you see those two things on the chair in the corner? Bring me the hexagon, not the triangle."

Bring me the hexagon, not the triangle.

Because children of this age already know what a triangle is, they quickly inferred that the hexagon must be the other shape and brought it to the experimenter.

A few minutes later the children were given a comprehension test (they were asked to point out the hexagon in a picture containing various shapes) and a production task (they were asked to name the shape). Once again, they did very well: they were able to pick out the right object on the comprehension test about three-quarters of the time, and they could say its name themselves about a third of the time. All of this after hearing the strange new word only once!

In another experiment, three- and four-year-old children were given a variety of objects to play with. The experimenter then casually introduced a new name for one of the objects, saying "Let's use the koba to measure which one is longer." And then, "We can put the koba away now." The children not only learned what *koba* meant, they remembered the new word a month later.[27]

How can children be this good and this fast? Sometimes, they get help from the situation in which they first hear the word. For instance, one study of family conversations at meal-time revealed that about two-thirds of the unfamiliar words that children encounter occur in situations that help make them understandable.[28] Sometimes, the situation even includes an explanation.

Mother: You want to wait a little while so you don't get cramps?
George (four years old): What's cramps?
Mother: Cramps are when your stomach . . . feels all tight . . . and it hurts 'cause you have food in it.

Often, though, the situation provides less direct clues about a word's meaning. For example, the following conversation introduces the word *rude* but leaves it up to the child to figure out precisely what it means.

Robert: (humming and talking with food in his mouth)
Mother: Robert
Catherine (four years old): Ma . . . can you please?
Mother: Robert, don't do that. That's rude.

In order to make do with the partial information that situations provide, children rely on various types of strategies that help them make good first guesses about a word's meaning. We'll look at those next.

4. Tools of the trade – how children learn nouns

Learning quickly is about making good initial guesses. Put simply, children are good word learners because they know what types of meanings to look for first. The strategies that guide them in the hunt for meaning can be roughly divided into four types – cognitive, social, linguistic, and organizational. Let's look at each type in turn.

Using your head (cognitive constraints)

Let's say a father is driving through the countryside with his eighteen-month-old daughter when he sees a sheep grazing by the side of the road. The father points to the animal and says "sheep." What is his child supposed to think the word means? Does it refer to the animal? Or just to part of the animal, perhaps its tail or its hooves? Does it perhaps mean "white" or "woolly?" Or does it refer to the fact that the animal is munching on grass? What's the best guess that a child can make under these circumstances?

By observing what children do in situations like this, we know that they follow a very simple and very sensible strategy known as the Whole Object Assumption.[29]

The Whole Object Assumption
A new word refers to a whole object.

So, the word *sheep* is taken to refer to the animal itself, not to its parts, not to its whiteness, and not to its woolliness.

So far so good, but what prevents a child from believing that *sheep* is not just the name of the particular animal she sees in front of her (just like "Fido" or "Spot" could be the name of a particular dog)? There's reason to think that children are guided by a second strategy, called the Type Assumption.[30]

The Type Assumption
A new word refers to a type of thing, not just to a particular individual.

So, *sheep* has to refer to a type of animal, not to just one particular sheep.

But there's still a problem. How is the child to know that *sheep* doesn't refer to animals in general? The answer to this question is a little subtler and involves the Basic Level Assumption.[31]

The Basic Level Assumption
A new word refers to types of objects that are alike in basic ways.

This means that all the things that *sheep* refers to should have obvious properties in common (shape, size, texture, and behavior) that aren't shared by other things.[32]

Three word-learning strategies for getting started

The Whole Object Assumption: A new word refers to a whole object.
The Type Assumption: A new word refers to a type of thing, not just to a particular individual.
The Basic Level Assumption: A new word refers to types of objects that are alike in basic ways.

These are very sensible strategies to follow and their effects are easy to observe – many of children's first nouns do in fact refer to types of objects that are alike in basic ways.

But these strategies can take the child only so far, since a lot of words refer to things other than whole objects. Sooner or later, children have to learn names for parts of things (like *toe*, *fingernail*, *belly button*, and so on), names for properties (*pretty*, *woolly*), names for individuals (like *Susie*, *Mr. Jones*), and names for very broad notions (like *animal* and *plant*). We'll talk more about this shortly.

Help from family and friends (social constraints)

We've already seen that the people around a child can help her learn the meaning of words in very tangible ways – perhaps by pointing to a particular object as they name it, or even by explaining what its meaning is. Much of language is picked up in a much subtler way, though, simply by listening to and being involved in conversations.

For children to benefit from this sort of experience, they have to have some sense of what other speakers are talking about. How can the meaning of a new word be learned if the speaker is referring to one thing and the child is focused on another? Somehow, children have to be "in sync" with other humans – noticing what they notice and thinking what they are thinking.

This is no trivial thing. In fact, psychologists often note that being able to sense the intentions and thoughts of others in this way involves having a "theory of mind" – an understanding of how other people's minds work. This is part of what it takes to be a social creature – to "fit in" to a family and a society.

The Social Strategy:
To figure out what new words mean, think like other people think.

A variety of experiments carried out by Michael Tomasello and his colleagues help illustrate this.[33]

In one experiment involving two-year-old children, an adult looked at and named a toy (saying, "Look! A modi!") just as the child's attention was drawn to another toy by lighting it up. When the children were then asked to retrieve the modi, they consistently chose the object that the adult had been looking at.

Somehow, the children knew that the adult was naming the toy that he was looking at when he spoke, regardless of what else was happening. That's the way language is used in ordinary social situations, and part of learning a language involves realizing that simple fact.

In another experiment, a child, her mother, and the experimenter played together with three novel objects. Then the mother left, and the experimenter brought out a *fourth* novel object, with which he and the child began to play. A little afterward, the mother returned to the room and exclaimed "Oh look! A modi! A modi!"

A subsequent comprehension task revealed that the children took *modi* to be the name of the fourth novel object. Somehow, they understood that the mother would not be excited about objects that she had previously played with, but that she could very well be excited by an object she was seeing for the first time. That's the way people are, and knowing that is an important part of being a human – and of understanding how language is used.

In a third experiment, the child was shown a curved pipe, down which things could be thrown. In one version of the experiment, an adult threw first one novel object down the pipe, and then another, before announcing "Now, modi!" as she threw a third novel object down. Children who watched this quickly concluded (as an adult no doubt would too) that *modi* was the name of the third novel object.

In another version of the experiment, the adult took out a novel object and first did one thing with it, and then another thing, and then announced "Now, modi!" as she threw it down the pipe. Children who saw this concluded that *modi* was the name of the action of throwing objects down a pipe.

In all these situations, the key to the child's success lies in "connecting" with another person in a fundamentally human way. The simple fact of the matter is that human beings talk about what they are thinking about. Being able to see what the speaker sees and being able to understand what he or she is thinking is not only a vital social skill, it is absolutely crucial for learning language as well.

Lessons from language (linguistic constraints)

Children also rely on what they've already learned about their language to learn new words. In one famous experiment, children were shown two dolls who were identical in appearance except for hair color (one was blonde, the other brunette).[34] The experimenter then talked about one of the dolls, referring to it either as "Zav" or as "a zav" several times. ("Look what I've brought you. This is Zav/a zav.") After a while, the children were told to "Dress Zav" or "Dress a zav."

Girls as young as seventeen months were able to notice the presence or absence of the little word *a*. (In this particular experiment, boys did not perform so well.) If they had been told that the first doll was Zav, they tended to dress that particular doll. But if they had been told that the first doll was "a zav," they were just as likely to dress the other doll. Evidently, they knew that *Zav* by itself was the name of a particular doll but that *a zav* refers to a *type* of doll.

Not bad for a one-and-a-half year old, but there's more. When the experiment was done using blocks rather than dolls, *a* no longer mattered. Regardless of whether they were asked to put away *Kiv* or *a kiv*, the children were just as likely to pick either block.

It seems that even very young children have figured out that dolls are more likely to have their own names than are inanimate blocks of wood. So, they paid attention to whether the experimenter used *a* when he was talking about dolls but not when he was talking about blocks. In effect, the children knew something that the experimenter seemed to be ignoring: you don't put a name on a block of wood.

Some clues take longer to pick up. Imagine, for example, that someone showed you a group of objects and said "This is a fendle."

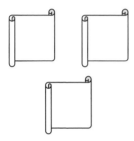

You would probably assume that *fendle* is the name for the entire *group* of objects, just as *flock* is the name for a group of birds. On the other hand, if you were told "These are fendles," you would probably conclude that each of the objects in the group is a fendle. Children can use the contrast between "a fendle" and "fendles" in the same way, but usually not until they are five years old.[35]

Also difficult is the contrast between nouns that denote solid substances and those that denote objects. You can think of a substance as something that passes the "grinder test" – unlike an object, its identity doesn't change even after it has been ground up. So wood is a substance, since it's still wood even after it's been ground up. On the other hand, a table is an object, since it would lose its identity if it were ground up.

All other things being equal, two- and three-year-olds prefer to interpret a noun that is used to refer to a solid object as the name of the object rather than the substance of which it is made. So if you point to a chair and say "mahogany," a child is likely to take *mahogany* to refer to the chair rather than the wood from which it is made.

The opposite tendency is found for non-solid substances such as liquids, powders, and gelatinous masses.[36] If you point to a mound of sawdust and say "mahogany," the word will probably be interpreted as the name of the substance itself rather than the name of whatever shape it forms.

In principle, the language should help children sort all of this out. That's because words like *some* and *much* commonly appear with nouns denoting substances, but not with nouns denoting objects.

Substance (OK with *some/much*)	Object (strange with *some/much*)
Some wood is in the kitchen.	**Some** table is in the kitchen.
How **much** wood is in the kitchen?	How **much** table is in the kitchen?

Are linguistic clues like these strong enough to override children's preference for nouns that name objects? Apparently not. In experiments where children have to decide whether a phrase such as *some lek* refers to an object or to the solid substance from which it is made, they tend to favor the object interpretation despite the linguistic clue pointing toward a substance interpretation.[37]

Being exclusive (an organizational constraint)

When you're faced with the prospects of learning the words for tens of thousands of concepts, it makes sense to look for ways to economize and keep things simple. One of the ways in which children do this is to adopt what Ellen Markman has called the Mutual Exclusivity Assumption.[38]

The Mutual Exclusivity Assumption
Things should have only one label.

One sign of Mutual Exclusivity in the early stages of language development is that children try to avoid calling things by more than one name. In conversations with parents, for example, two-year-olds have been observed to insist that something is a Cadillac but not a car,[39] or that it is a "jet-plane" but not a plane,[40] and so forth. They just can't seem to bear the thought that something could be called by more than one name.

This in turn affects children's ability to deal with class inclusion – to realize for instance that if something is a dog, it is also an animal. In one experiment, for example, children were asked questions such as:[41]

A pug is a kind of dog. Does a pug have to be an animal?

In order to give a correct "yes" answer, a child needs to understand that anything that is a dog is also an animal. That is, dogs are a subclass of animals.

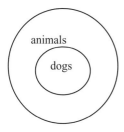

Six-year-olds do very well on these types of questions and often respond correctly 90 percent of the time. However, four-year-olds do considerably less well, often scoring in the 60 percent range. This is presumably because the Mutual Exclusivity Assumption interferes with their ability to recognize that something can be both a dog and an animal at the same time.

Another manifestation of Mutual Exclusivity can be seen in children's tendency to treat new words as names for objects that don't yet have names – as in the triangle/hexagon experiment discussed earlier (section 3). A slightly different version of this experiment makes use of nonsense words in order to ensure that children have had no prior exposure to the test items.

Three-year-old children are shown a pair of pictures, one of a familiar object (say, a tree) and the other of an unfamiliar object (say, a car muffler). They are then asked "Show me the zib."[42]

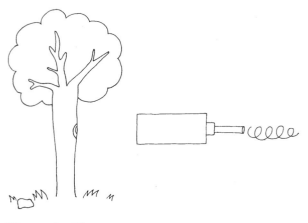

"Show me the zib"

Under these circumstances, children exhibit an overwhelming tendency to assume that the novel word goes with the object for which they don't already have a name. So, when asked to point to the "zib," they pick the muffler five times out of six on average. (When asked to pick an object without being given a name, they choose the unfamiliar object only about half the time.)

Mutual Exclusivity works well for children's early vocabulary – things that are dogs cannot also be cats, things that are cars cannot also be boats, and so on. It may also be helpful when it comes to putting the brakes on the Whole Object Assumption, which leads children to assume that a new word is the name for a whole object, not just for its parts, or its color, or its texture.

As we saw a bit earlier, this assumption has to be overridden at some point, since there are words like *nose* and *toe* that refer to parts, words like *dark* and *white* that refer to colors, words like *soft* and *woolly* that refer to texture, and so forth. Mutual Exclusivity may provide children with a way to do this. Let's consider a concrete example.

Imagine that you are looking at a book with a child and that you come across a picture of a rabbit. You point to it and say "fluffy." If the child already knows the word *rabbit*, the Mutual Exclusivity Assumption will prevent her from thinking that *fluffy* means "rabbit," since she already has a word with that meaning. So, she's got to assume that the new word refers to something else associated with rabbits, in this case their texture.[43]

So far, we've been concentrating on how children learn the meanings of nouns. But in addition to the thing-type meanings associated with nouns, a child also has to learn the action-type meanings expressed by verbs (*run, fall, eat*), the property-type meanings that go with adjectives (*big, hungry, sore*), and the relational meanings expressed by prepositions (*in, on, under*). Let's have a quick look at each.

5. Learning verbs

Despite their early love of nouns, children are good verb-learners. A detailed diary study of one child (Damon) revealed that he used 94 different verbs by age two and 321 different verbs by age three.[44]

In general, the first verbs children learn are the ones they hear most frequently in the speech of their parents.[45] Among Damon's very first verbs were the "general purpose" items *do, get, go,* and *put*.

do:	I do that
	Me do brush
get:	get down
	get that
	get off
	get a cracker
	I get drink
	get on
	get down off
go:	go down
	go?
	this one go bye
	baby go boom
	go swimming
	go watch car
put:	put back
	put ball
	put there
	put on
	put them more
	put down floor
	put it back
	put it up!

The most common type of verb in Damon's speech denoted *activities* – actions like running, playing, riding, and reading that have no particular endpoint. More than half of his verbs were of this type up to age three.

The second most common type of verb (more than a third of Damon's total) denoted *accomplishments*. These are actions that have a clear end point and that typically bring about a particular result – finding something, knocking down a pile of blocks, tearing something out of a newspaper.

Percentage of verbs by type[46]

Age (months)	Activities (%)	Accomplishments (%)	Others (%)
19–24	55	32	13
25–30	48	36	16
31–36	47	39	14

Similar findings have been reported for other children.

A number of researchers have reported that particular verb forms are more likely to show up with particular types of verbs than with others. For example, about 90 percent of all -*ing* endings in Damon's speech prior to age three show up on activity verbs.

> Mommy eating.
> I playing.

At the same time, past tense inflection is most likely to appear on accomplishment verbs.[47]

> I found it.
> It fell.
> It broke.

Very young children seem to associate the past tense form of a verb with a completed act and are confused when a past action is incomplete. That's why two-year-olds often interpret sentences such as *The girl WAS drawing a picture* to mean "is drawing," if the picture has not been completed. Four-year-olds don't have this problem distinguishing between the time of an event and its completeness.[48]

Bootstrapping

Verb meanings are often quite abstract, which raises the question of just how children figure them out. One thing that may help is noticing the particular "frame" in which a new verb occurs. Imagine, for example, that you hear the following sentence.

Mary FLUMPED them to her father.

Even though you've just encountered *flump* for the first time in your life, you can make an educated guess about its meaning from the frame in which it occurs – it must involve transferring things to the possession of another person.

Now try to figure out the meaning of *zwig* by looking at the frame in which it occurs in the following sentence.

Daddy ZWIGS that we should have spaghetti for supper.

Given its syntactic frame, *zwig* must denote either an act of communication like *say* or a mental state like *think*, *know*, or *believe*.

Using information like this to make a first guess at a word's meaning is called "syntactic bootstrapping." You've probably heard the expression "he pulled himself up by his bootstraps." In the case of meaning, the bootstrap corresponds to the "frame" in which the word occurs.

A concrete example of how children use a language's bootstraps to learn a verb's meaning comes from an experiment involving two-year-old children and pictures like the ones below.

When the children hear the sentence "The monkey is flexing the bunny," they tend to look at the picture on the left, where the monkey is doing something to the rabbit.

On the other hand, if they hear the sentence "The monkey is flexing WITH the bunny," they tend to look at the picture on the right, in which the monkey and the rabbit are looking and pointing in the same direction.

How does this happen? Evidently, children know that the *noun–verb–noun* frame is best suited to a meaning in which one animal acts on the other, while the frame containing *with* is better for situations in which the two animals act together.[49] By taking the verb's syntactic frame as their starting point, they are able to infer its meaning – syntactic bootstrapping in action.

Some tough verbs

Of course, syntactic bootstrapping does no more than get children started. Somehow, they must still figure out the differences in meaning among verbs such as *think*, *know*, and *believe*, all of which can occur in the same type of frame. That can't be easy. After all, a person looks exactly the same regardless of whether she's thinking, knowing, or believing. That may be why the acquisition of verbs describing mental states and processes can be quite slow. Take the verb *forget*, for example.

When you and I say that we forgot to do something, we are saying both that we knew at one time that we were supposed to do that thing and that we did not remember to do it. However, the results of a simple experiment suggest that failure to remember is not an essential part of the meaning of *forget* in the view of young children.

In the experiment, children aged four to seven listened to stories like the one below.[50]

> One day Tom's mother asks Tom to go to the store and buy some apples. She gives him some money and a basket. Sarah's mother also wants some apples and she gives Sarah some money and a basket and asks her to buy some apples as well.

When Tom gets to the store, he finds that he has lost his money. So he goes home.

When Sarah gets to the store, she sees the library and goes in there instead and reads some books. And then she goes home.

After being asked a series of questions to make sure that they understood the story, the children heard the key question: "Who forgot to buy apples?"

Now, an adult would say that Sarah forgot – she knew she was supposed to buy apples, but because she was distracted by the library she didn't remember and went home without them. We wouldn't say that Tom forgot, though. His problem was just that he lost the money.

But that's not the way preschool children see things: their most common response was to say that both Tom and Sarah forgot! For them, *forget* seems to mean not "fail to recall," but rather "fail to fulfill one's original intention."

Children also seem puzzled by the verb *promise*, as shown by their reaction to the following two stories.

Corrinda and Nevin are playing in the park. Corrinda said, "Let's go play on the swings." Nevin said, "I will later. But now I have to go home for lunch." Then Nevin said, "We will play on the swings when I come back, I promise." After Nevin ate lunch, he felt so sick that he just had to lie down. Nevin didn't come back to the park. Corrinda went to his house to find him. Nevin's mom told Corrinda that Nevin was sick.

Danny and Emily are at school helping their teacher. Danny said, "We should erase the chalkboard next." Emily said, "Yeah! But first I better put my homework in my locker." Then Emily said, "We will erase the chalkboard when I come back, I promise." Emily went to her locker. It was such a nice day that Emily decided to go home so she could play. Emily didn't come back to help Danny. Danny waited for Emily to come back. He saw Emily skipping down the sidewalk.

Both seven-year-olds and nine-year-olds recognize that Nevin is not to be blamed for what happened, but that Emily is. However, many seven-year-olds insist that neither Nevin nor Emily made a promise.[51] Apparently they miss an essential fact about promising, which is that it involves a verbal commitment without regard for subsequent distractions and obstacles.

Another verb that can cause trouble is *fill*. Many preschool children believe that *fill* means "pour" rather than "make full." So, when they are asked to decide which of the two series of pictures below is an example of filling, they choose the second series – even though the glass ends up empty![52]

Interestingly, there is a tendency for four- and five-year-old children who are confused in this way about the meaning of *fill* to use it in patterns where it just doesn't fit by adult standards.[53]

> And fill the little sugars up in the bowl . . . (Mark, at age 4;7 [4;7 stands for four years seven months])
> Can I fill some salt into the [salt shaker]? (E, at age 5)
> I filled the grain up. (Adam, at age 4;11)

These errors disappear as children come to realize that *fill* means "make full" rather than "pour into."

6. Learning adjectives

Parents use fewer adjectives (descriptive words such as *big* or *red*) than nouns or verbs when speaking to children, so it's perhaps not surprising that adjectives tend to be acquired later.[54] The ideal situation for learning an adjective seems to arise when it is used for objects that are either different in just one way or similar in just one way.

In an intriguing experiment, three-year-old children were shown two plates – one transparent and the other opaque. When told that the transparent plate was "blickish" but that the opaque plate was not, they quickly learned that *blickish* meant "transparent," apparently because the two objects differed in just that one way.

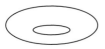

This is blickish.

This is not blickish.

But when the children were shown a transparent plate and an opaque toothbrush (objects that are different in many ways), they couldn't figure out what *blickish* meant.

This is blickish.

This is not blickish.

In another version of the experiment, the children were shown a transparent plate and a transparent toothbrush (two objects that have just one thing in common), and were told that each was "blickish."

This is blickish.   *This is blickish.*

Under these circumstances they succeeded in figuring out what *blickish* meant.

But they were far less successful when they were shown two transparent plates (objects that were similar in many ways) and told that each was "blickish."[55]

This is blickish.   *This is blickish.*

Learning new adjectives

Learning the meaning of a new adjective is easy when it is used to describe:

a. an object that differs from another object in just one way, or
b. two objects that are alike in just one way

Of course, such ideal situations do not arise all that often in real life, which may be why parents are more likely to explain adjective meanings than noun meanings to their children.[56]

The first two types of adjectives acquired by most children are words describing sizes (*big, small, tall*) and colors (*red, blue, green*). Let's look at each case.

Sizes

Size words in English express a number of subtle contrasts, as you can see if you think about the meaning of *big, tall,* and *long.* The first word is used for overall size, the second for size on a vertical dimension, and the third for size on the horizontal dimension.

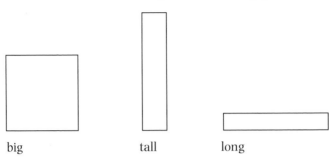

big   tall   long

And that's just for starters – words like *high*, *wide*, and *deep* have to be figured out as well.

In one experiment investigating the acquisition of size words, children aged three to five were shown pairs of objects – sometimes a big one and a tall one, sometimes a big one and a long one, and sometimes a tall one and a long one.[57]

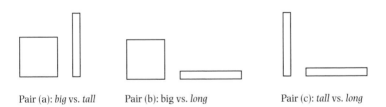

Pair (a): *big* vs. *tall*   Pair (b): *big* vs. *long*   Pair (c): *tall* vs. *long*

The younger children in the experiment did fine when asked to choose "the big one." However, they did much less well when asked to choose "the tall one" or "the long one"; in fact, they often picked the big one instead. Evidently, they were more sensitive to overall size than to a single dimension like height or length.

More than half of the older children had a different problem. They did less well on "big," which they tended to equate with "tall." So, when asked to select the "big one" in pair (a), they would select the object on the right. This suggests they were focusing on the vertical dimension in making judgments about size.

Size adjectives are complicated in another way as well – their precise meaning is often relative. "Big" for a mouse is not the same thing as "big" for an elephant. And whereas "big" usually refers to height when it describes a person, it typically refers to overall size when applied to houses.

Children (and even adults) can have trouble with this, especially when there are conflicting criteria – as when they have to decide whether a large doll counts as a small toy.[58]

Colors

Children have great difficulty learning their first color words, but not because they can't SEE the difference between colors. A two-year-old who is given a red toy can retrieve it later even if it is put with an identical toy of a different color.[59]

Yet in experiments where researchers try to teach two-year-olds a first color word, dozens of attempts are necessary.[60] This is obviously a far cry from fast mapping.

Many studies have reported that color words aren't used appropriately until around age four or later – in sharp contrast to names for shapes, which are acquired much earlier.[61] Three-year-olds who are asked "What color is this?" typically respond with a color name, but they either use the same name (red, say) for all colors or randomly choose among color names.[62]

Interestingly, however, at least one recent study reports that today's two-and-a-half-year-olds have considerable knowledge of color terms. Some researchers think this may be due to increased exposure to color names through television and preschool.[63]

The acquisition of color terms differs from the acquisition of names for things found in nature, such as animals. Although preschool children do equally well on high-frequency color terms (e.g., *red* and *blue*) and animal names (*cow* and *bear*), a difference shows up on low-frequency items. Here, children do far better on animal names such as *platypus* and *scorpion* than on color terms such as *beige* and *violet*.[64]

This may be because the referents of color terms overlap to some extent – the line between "green" and "olive," or "purple" and "violet" is just not that clear.[65] There's no similar chance of confusion with animal names, since the boundary between notions such as "cat" and "dog" is sharp and clear-cut.

The most spectacular attempt to study the development of color names in children (and one of the largest-scale studies ever of child language) was an experiment involving 669 children aged two and a half to four and a half.[66] The children were shown colored pieces of paper (in different orders) and asked to name them.

The average success rates for each color revealed the following developmental order for the use of color names. (Similar results have been reported for the comprehension of color words.)[67]

red green black white orange yellow blue pink brown purple

One of the things that makes this study especially interesting is that the first color names learned by the children were for the hues that are most often distinguished in languages and cultures the world over – red, green, black, and white. These are evidently colors that catch the human eye, calling out for attention and for a name.

Numbers

Finally, a word on numbers is in order. Although many children learn to count to ten as early as age two, they seem not to understand the actual meaning of the numbers they use until they are three and a half years old or so.

A two- or three-year-old who is seated in front of a dozen toy animals and asked to put five of them in a separate pile will often pick an incorrect number, even if she's perfectly able to count to five. And when asked to count the animals in the new pile, she'll often modify the way she counts so as to get the right answer. So, if she has put just three animals in the pile, she'll count them by saying "one, two, five"![68]

Children learn the meaning of number words in a more or less fixed manner – first one, of course, and then two and three. (Three is the maximum number of entities whose quantity can reliably be ascertained without actual counting.)

The next step, which occurs around age three and a half is the big one: children simultaneously learn the meaning of all the remaining numbers that they know. This is also the time at which they finally figure out that counting determines the number of things in a set – that the way to determine that there are five candles on the cake is to count them in a sequence from one to five.[69]

Sometime around age four to six, children learn a second number sequence – 20, 30, 40, and so on, which they combine with their knowledge of the numbers one to nine to greatly expand their range of counting. Here's an example from Deborah and Rebecca, twins who are about to turn five.[70]

> Deborah: 1, 2, 3, 4, 5, 6, 7, 8, 9, 10, 11, 12, 13, 14, 15, 16, 17, 18, 19.
> Rebecca (to her mother): What's after 19?
> Mother: 20
> Rebecca: 21, 22, 23, 24, 25, 26, 27, 28, 29. What's after?
> Mother: 30.
> Rebecca: 31, 32, 33, 34, 35, 36, 37, 38, 39. Now 40.

7. Learning prepositions

Prepositions are used to indicate relations between words. Some of these relations involve position and direction (*in, toward, near*). Others are more abstract and involve notions like benefit (*for*), instrument (*with*), and possession (*of*).

Some notions expressed by prepositions

> *location*: Sleep **in** your own bed. The ball is **on** the floor.
> *origin*: He came **from** China.
> *direction*: Let's walk **down** the hill. The bug climbs **up** the wall.
> *accompaniment*: Go **with** your mom.
> *benefit*: Would you get that **for** me?
> *instrument/means*: Cut it **with** the scissors. We'll go **by** car.
> *possession/belonging*: That toy **of** mine.

Children's first prepositions carry much the same information as street signs – they express locations and directions.[71]

First prepositions in the speech of a one-year-old girl

Preposition	Age of first use (months)
up	17
down	17
on	18
off	18
in	18
out	18
over	19
under	19

Besides being very useful, these particular prepositions have another thing going for them: they are very noticeable in English. That's because they can occur at the ends of sentences, where they can carry stress and are therefore doubly salient to children.

I want UP/DOWN/IN/OUT.
I want this sweater ON/OFF.

Initially, children may use prepositions to express actions rather than relations. For example, *down* is used to mean "fall down" or "put me down," *in* is used to mean "let's go inside," and so on.

Even after prepositions take on a relational meaning, two types of errors are common – one involving omission and the other involving commission.

Errors of omission and commission

Omission errors occur when children fail to use a preposition where one is called for.

Draw paper. (for "Draw on paper.")
Ketchup mouth. (for "Ketchup in mouth.")
Peter hurt car. (for "Peter was hurt by a car.")
Open it keys. (for "Open it with keys.")

Such errors may arise because of a lag between the ability to conceive of a particular relation (location, instrument, direction) and the ability to express it.

Judith Johnston and Dan Slobin have suggested a very apt metaphor for this: notions must sometimes be held in the mind's "waiting room" until the arrival of the words that can be used to express them.[72] When preposition-type meanings are stuck in the waiting room, children end up producing sentences like *Ketchup mouth* and *Open it keys*.

Errors of commission take place when a wrong preposition is used. The two most common errors of this type involve using *for* in place of *to* and *by* instead of instrumental *with*.

> Timothy gave that FOR me. (instead of "to me")
> Santa Claus gave that lollipop FOR me. (instead of "to me")
> Crack pecan BY teeth. (instead of "with teeth")
> Can I pick it up BY my hands? (instead of "with my hands")

Among prepositions expressing location, some seem easier than others. In one study, children aged two to four were asked to describe the position of a small object such as a stone with respect to a larger object such as a plate.[73]

 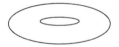 

The first prepositions to be used were *in*, *on*, *under*, and *beside*, all of which indicate a simple spatial relationship between two objects. These were followed by *between*, which is slightly more complicated since it indicates a relationship between one object and two others.

Harder still are *in front of* and *behind* when they were used with objects such as TVs and houses – since the speaker has to pay attention to the relationship between one object and PART of another (its front or its back).

Hardest of all are these same prepositions when they are used with objects, such as bottles and boxes, that have no inherent front or back. Under such circumstances, speakers have to take into account their own position with respect to the two objects in order to decide which preposition to use.

If a ball is between me and a box, I'll say that it is "in front of" the box. But if the box is between me and the ball, I'll say that the ball is "behind the box."

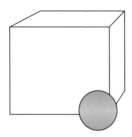 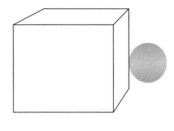

"The ball is in front of the box."   "The ball is behind the box."

Having to take one's own position into account in choosing a preposition complicates matters even more, further delaying the acquisition of *in front of* and *behind*.

Common developmental order for prepositions expressing location

Preposition	Type of relation expressed
in, on, under, beside	a simple spatial relation between two objects
between	a spatial relation between one object and two others
in front of, behind	a relation between one object and another with an inherent front and back
in front of, behind	a relationship between one object and another with no inherent front or back

8. Learning pronouns: *I* and *you*

One of the most noticeable meaning errors in early multi-word speech involves the confusion of *I* (or *me*) and *you*. Here are some errors from the speech of two-year-old Matthew.[74]

I'll carry you. (for 'YOU carry ME.')
You'll cry. (for 'I'LL cry.')
Lift you up and you can see out the window. (for 'Lift ME up and I can see out the window.')

Pronoun reversals like this are a quite common occurrence. One study of eighteen-month-old children revealed that more than half reversed pronouns some of the time.[75] And many others avoided using pronouns altogether in favor of names – they said things like "Mommy go there" rather than "You go there" when speaking to their mother.

It's not hard to see why words like *I* and *you* might be confusing for a child. Think about how you speak to a child. You use *I* to refer to yourself, but the child is expected to use that word to refer to herself. And you use *you* to refer to the child, but she is expected to use it to refer to you!

I'm here. You're there.

Nonetheless, it is important to recognize that children tend to be confused rather than fundamentally mistaken about how pronouns work. Even the most hard-core "reversers" seem to make mistakes no more than half the time.[76]

Errors are considerably more common with *you* than with *I* – that is, a child is more likely to use *you* to refer to herself than she is to say *I* to refer to someone else.[77] This is perhaps because everyone who speaks to the child is likely to address her as "you" while referring to themselves as "I." This makes it easy for the child to figure out that *I* is used for any speaker, but it could encourage her to use *you* to refer to herself.

If this is right, then children should figure out pronouns more easily if they frequently hear others addressed as "you" too. And, in fact, we have a fascinating clue that this does help: second-born children seem to produce correct pronouns earlier than first-borns, presumably because they have the advantage of seeing *you* modeled with an older sibling.[78]

Is it harder for children to keep *I* and *you* straight when they're speaking or when they're listening? A simple experiment helps reveal the answer. Holding a toy (say, a ball) in her hand, the experimenter gives another toy (say, a doll) to the child and then asks:

"What do I have?"
"What do you have?"
"Do I have the ball?"
"Do you have the ball?"
"Is the doll mine?"
"Is the ball yours?"
"Is it my ball?"
"Is it your doll?"

In order to test the child's ability to make these distinctions in her own speech, the experimenter can ask the following questions.

"Who has the ball?"
"Who has the doll?"
"Whose ball is it?"
"Whose doll is it?"

When this experiment was done with two- and three-year-old children, there were far more instances of *I/you* confusion on the questions testing comprehension.[79]

This same study included a series of simple tasks designed to investigate a possible connection between children's understanding of the *I/you* distinction and their ability to take the perspective of another person. In one such task, the child was given a large poster with a picture of (say) the sun on one side and a picture of a heart on the other. She was shown both sides repeatedly until she could say which picture was on each side without looking. Then, as she looked at one side of the poster, she was asked what an adult on the other side of the poster could see.

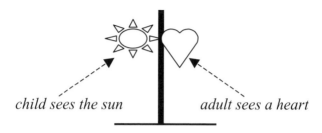

child sees the sun   *adult sees a heart*

The child is asked, "What does the other person see?"

Children who were able to take the perspective of the other person named the picture on the opposite side of the poster rather than the one on their own side.

The perspective-shifting skill required here is similar to the point of view contrasts involved in the use of *I* and *you*: a child has to realize that although she should call herself "I" and others "you," others will use "I" for themselves and "you" for her when it's their turn to talk. And, sure enough, only children who did well on the perspective-shifting task seem to have fully mastered the *I/you* distinction.[80]

Summing up

Children are able to identify the meanings of new words with stunning speed and accuracy. They can learn one or two words an hour week after week and month after month, often after hearing them only once (fast mapping). There are mistakes, primarily overextensions, especially in the first year or two, but children's overall performance as word learners is extremely impressive. There is still much that we do not understand about all of this, but there is good reason to think that children's abilities as word learners are largely due to the simple strategies talked about in this chapter.

The next thing to think about has to do with how children are able to put together words to make sentences. This too is an essential part of the language learning process. We couldn't build sentences without words, but words by themselves are a lot like a stack of building material. Their real value comes from the fact that they can be assembled in particular ways to create the sentence-sized structures that we use to communicate with each other. How children learn to do this is the topic for our next chapter.

4 Words all in a row

Imagine for a moment what it would be like to have words, but no systematic way to combine them. You'd have to communicate in tiny one-word installments – "thirsty," "water," "give." That must be roughly what it's like to be a fifteen-month-old child with something to say.

There's considerable incentive, then, for children to learn how to create sentences, and it doesn't take them long to get started, as we'll see. The development of children's sentence-building skills can be roughly divided into two phases.

The first phase, which begins around the age of eighteen months, sees the appearance of relatively simple two- and three-word patterns. These early sentences are primitive and often incomplete, but they mark the start of something big.

During the second phase, which begins around age two or so, the missing pieces are filled in and there is rapid growth in the ability to produce a wide variety of complex constructions.

1. Getting started

The basic recipe for sentence building is simple: Combine two words with the right fit (say, an adjective and a noun, or a noun and a verb) in the right order. Repeat the process as many times as necessary, adding one new word or combination of words each time.

Take, for example, the sentence *The glass broke*. You start with the words *the* and *glass*, and combine them to create the phrase *the glass*.

the   glass

Then you combine that phrase with the verb *broke*.

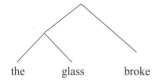

the   glass   broke

Sentences are like (upside-down) trees whose branches can sprout outward endlessly, so that there's no limit on how long a sentence can be. Even children's bedtime stories sometimes capitalize on this fact – remember the dog that chased the cat that caught the mouse that ate the cheese in the house that Jack built? A language's sentence-building machinery lets you say what you want to say, no matter how lengthy or complex or devious your message is.

Grammar in the cradle?

Even very young children seem to have a natural ability to recognize recurring patterns in speech. A very striking illustration of this comes from an experiment conducted by Gary Marcus and his colleagues.[1] They began by familiarizing seven-month-old infants with a two-minute speech sample that contained three repetitions of various three-word "sentences" consisting of nonsense syllables. Here are two examples:

> ga ga ti . . . ga ga ti . . . ga ga ti
> li li na , , , li li na . . . li li na

These particular sentences follow an XXY pattern since they consist of two identical syllables followed by a new syllable.

Next, the infants were presented with twelve new sentences. Half of these involved new instances of the XXY pattern (perhaps *bo bo na* or *re re nu*). The other half involved an unfamiliar XYY pattern in which the final two syllables were identical and the first syllable was different – *fe wo wo* and *ta gi gi*, for example.

All sixteen infants looked longer at the source of the voice during the presentation of the new pattern than during presentation of the familiar pattern. Somehow they recognized that *bo bo na* was like *ga ga ti* and *li li na*, while *fe wo wo* was new and more interesting. This sort of ability may be useful for identifying the patterns that make up sentences too.

In fact, there is evidence that children are aware of various grammatical patterns well before they produce them themselves. In one particularly intriguing experiment, Lynn Santelmann and Peter Jusczyk had fifteen- and eighteen-month-old children listen to passages containing *is + V-ing* patterns (such as *is baking*) and to passages containing ill-formed *can + V-ing* patterns (such as *can baking*). Here are parts of two sample passages.

is + V-ing	*can + V-ing*
At the bakery, everyone IS BAKING bread. One person IS MIXING the flour and water together. Someone else IS ADDING salt and yeast. In the next room, a machine IS KNEADING the dough . . .	At the bakery, everyone CAN BAKING bread. One person CAN MIXING the flour and water together. Someone else CAN ADDING salt and yeast. In the next room, a machine CAN KNEADING the dough . . .

Although neither group of children had begun to produce *is + V-ing* patterns in their own speech, the eighteen-month-olds listened longer to the passage containing the *is + V-ing* pattern than to the *can + V-ing* pattern. Evidently they recognized the *is + V-ing* pattern as part of their language.[2]

Real words and real sentences

Most children begin combining words in their own speech some time between the ages of eighteen and twenty-four months, at about the time they have vocabularies of around fifty words or so.

Damon is typical in this respect, as you can see by considering the following graph, but some children begin sooner and others later.

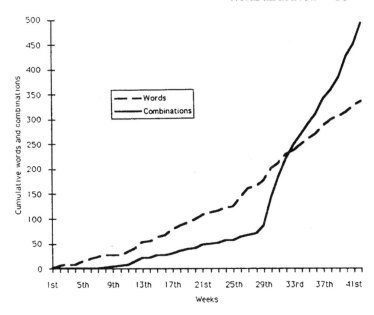

Damon reached the fifty-word milestone around the thirteenth week of the study, when he was about fifteen months old. At about this time, the number of word combinations (represented by the solid line) began to increase, first slowly and then much more rapidly. By the end of the nine-month study, Damon had produced almost five hundred different sentences.

Tracking the growth of sentences

One of the ways that linguists keep track of sentence growth is to calculate a child's *MLU* – or *mean length of utterance*. This is done by determining the average number of meaning-bearing elements (or *morphemes*, to use the technical term) in his sentences. In Adam's sentence *Play checkers*, for instance, there are three such elements – *play*, *checker*, and the plural suffix -*s*. (Appendix 1 contains some additional information about how MLU is calculated.)

Over time, a child's MLU increases steadily, at an average rate of 1.25 morphemes per year according to one large-scale study.[3]

The following graph depicts growth in the MLU of Adam, Eve, and Sarah, three children who were studied by researchers at Harvard and whose names have become household words to acquisition researchers.[4]

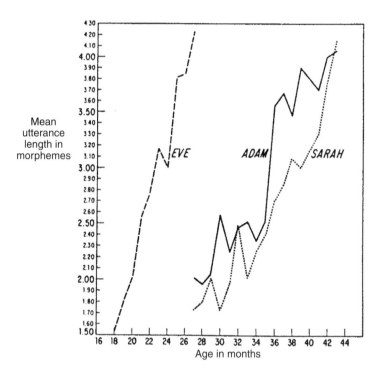

One of the things that you may notice here is that Eve develops much faster than the other two children. Her MLU is above three morphemes by the time she is two years old – almost a full year before Adam and Sarah reach that level. All of which underlines the point that some children develop more quickly than others and that variation from child to child in the rate of language learning is not normally a cause for concern.

How are increases in MLU reflected in children's actual speech? Take a look at the following snapshots (from Steven Pinker) of Adam's language over a mere eleven months.[5]

Sample utterances from Adam's speech over a twelve-month period

Age (months)	Sample utterances
27	Play checkers.
	Big drum.
	I got horn.
	A bunny-rabbit walk.
30	Write a piece a paper.
	What that egg doing?
	I lost a shoe.
	No, I don't want to sit seat.
32	Let me get down with the boots on.
	Don't be afraid a horses.
	How tiger be so healthy and fly like kite?
	Joshua throw like penguin.
34	Look at that train Ursula brought.
	I simply don't want put in chair.
	Don't have paper.
	Do you want little bit, Cromer?
	I can't wear it tomorrow.
36	I going come in fourteen minutes.
	I going wear that to wedding.
	I see what happens.
	I have to save them now.
	Those are not strong mens.
	They are going sleep in wintertime.
	You dress me up like a baby elephant.
38	So it can't be cleaned?
	I broke my racing car.
	Do you know the lights went off?
	What happened to the bridge?
	Can I put my head in the mailbox so the mailman can know where I are and put me in the mailbox?

The growth here is truly remarkable. The sentences get longer. Words such as *the* and *is* that previously had been missing make their appearance. Various patterns of negation show up (*don't*, *can't*, *am not*). And a variety of question types are used (*Do you know . . . ?*, *Can I put . . . ?*, *What happened . . . ?*).

These developments call for a closer look. We'll start by considering the design of children's early utterances, investigating how the parts are arranged, what's there, and what's missing. Then we'll examine a series of more complicated sentence types (including negatives, questions, and relative clauses) that are an essential part of speaking and understanding a language.

2. Pivotal words

Children's first sentences are mostly two words in length. The following typical examples are from a child named Gregory.[6]

see boy	push it	allgone shoe
see sock	move it	allgone egg
see hot	close it	allgone watch
	do it	allgone vitamins

Many of children's early sentences seem to be built around a small number of *pivot words* that serve as hooks to which other words can be attached. In the examples above, *see, it*, and *allgone* are the pivots: they show up over and over again in the company of a variety of different words.

Before long, sentences containing three or more words make their appearance, often around the age of twenty-five months. The transition can be rapid – it's not unusual to see the proportion of these longer sentences increase from less than 15 percent of a child's total output to more than 50 percent in the space of just a few weeks.[7]

Once again, though, there is evidence that learning is initially "item-based." In a very large number of cases, children seem to exploit a "cut-and-paste" strategy that puts new words into slots in pre-made frames such as *Where's the X, Put X here*, and so on.[8]

Where's the X	I wanna X	It's a X
Where's the ball?	I wanna go.	It's a mouse.
Where's the book?	I wanna watch TV.	It's a toy car.

I'm X-ing it	Put X here	Let's X it.
I'm doing it.	Put dolly here.	Let's wash it.
I'm cleaning it.	Put milk here.	Let's drink it.

Verbs are the nuclei around which most longer sentences are built. In fact, the choice of a verb goes a long way toward determining what other types of words are going to be present in the sentence.

If the verb is *push*, you expect two nouns or pronouns in the sentence – one for the person who does the pushing and one for the person or thing that is pushed.

   1   2
You can PUSH the carriage.

If the verb is *give*, you'll expect three nouns or pronouns – one for the giver, one for the thing that is given, and one for the recipient.

   1   2 3
Mommy will GIVE you juice.

And if the verb is *fall*, there is likely to be only one person involved.

   1
She FELL.

Children themselves seem to realize the importance of verbs, and they are very cautious about handling them. Initially, children may use a new verb only in the particular way that they have heard it used. In contrast, when they learn a new noun, they immediately begin to use it in a variety of ways – in the singular and in the plural, as a "doer" and as an "undergoer."[9]

So a child who hears the sentence *They assembled the shed* is likely to be cautious about using *assemble* in new contexts. It is unlikely that she would say *The shed assembled*, for instance. But she won't hesitate to assume that *shed* has the plural form *sheds* and that it can occur in other positions in a sentence, as in *We need a new shed* or *There's a caterpillar in the shed*.

With time, children's sentence-building becomes more creative and open-ended. A wider variety of structural patterns make their appearance, and verbs are used more freely. One of the things that makes all of this possible is the emergence of general "rules" for combining and arranging items in the proper order. We'll look at that next.

3. Getting things lined up

Every language has a strategy for distinguishing between a subject (usually the "doer") and a direct object (the "undergoer"). Otherwise, there'd be no way to know the meaning of *The car pushed the truck* – it could mean either that the car does the pushing or that the truck does. English adopts a simple solution to this problem: it puts the subject in front of the verb and the direct object after it.

The car	pushed	the truck.
subject	verb	direct object
(doer)		(undergoer)

So *The car pushed the truck* has to mean that the car does the pushing and that the truck gets pushed.

Children seem to have very little trouble with word order in their own speech – they use the correct order around 95 percent of the time or more, even in their earliest sentences.[10] One minor exception to this is the occasional use of a verb-subject order in sentences where there is no direct object. Here are some examples, along with the names and ages of the children who produced them.[11] (1;10 stands for one year, ten months old; and so on.)

Going it. (Naomi, 1;10)
Going (re)corder. (Naomi, 1;10)
Come car. (Eve, 1;6)
Came a man. (Eve, 1;8)
Fall pants. (Nina, 1;11)
Fall down lady. (Nina, 1;11)
Come Lois. (Peter, 2;1)
Broken the light. (Peter, 2;2)

Such verb-first sentences are typically quite rare and seem to be possible only when the verb describes movement (such as coming, going or falling) or a change of state (breaking). Verbs like *jump* and *eat* don't show up in front of their subject.

Big rules and little rules

How do children manage to do so well with word order? One possibility is that they learn one big rule that says something like "Always put the subject in front of the verb."

Another possibility is that they learn a lot of little rules – one for each verb – that say "Put the subject in front of *push*"; "Put the subject in front of *read*"; "Put the subject in front of *eat*"; and so on.

A "big rule"	"Little rules"
Put the subject in front of the verb.	Put the subject in front of *push* Put the subject in front of *read* Put the subject in front of *eat* . . .

We know that adults have the big rule because whenever they learn a new verb, they automatically know that the subject is going to come in front of it. However, an experiment by Nameera Akhtar suggests that children may start out with little rules.[12]

Children aged two to four were taught three made-up verbs (*tam, gop,* and *dack*) for three novel actions involving puppet characters. One verb was presented in each of the following orders:

subject–verb–object order:
Elmo *tammed* the apple. (the usual order for English)
subject–object–verb order:
Elmo the apple *gopped*. (not permitted in "real" English)
verb–object–subject order:
Dacked the apple Elmo. (not permitted in "real" English)

When describing the actions themselves, the two- and three-year-old children were willing to use word order patterns not found in English. For example, they'd say "Dacked the apple Elmo" about half the time if that's the way they'd heard the experimenter say it. It seems that they were learning a little rule for each new verb and didn't yet realize that *all* verbs come after the subject in English.

The four-year-olds were different, though. Regardless of the word order pattern in which they heard a new verb, they'd put it into a subject–verb–direct object order when they used it themselves. That's because, like adults, they have a big rule that says English word order is subject + verb + direct object – regardless of what the verb is.

4. Missing big pieces

Although subjects, verbs, and direct objects are vital pieces of sentences, they are sometimes missing in early child language.

Missing subject
    _ see boy.
    _ helping Mommy.
Missing verb
    Ken _ water. (= Ken is drinking water)
    Eve _ lunch. (= Eve is eating lunch)
Missing direct object
    Lady do _.
    Man taking _.

Sentences with missing verbs are rather rare,[13] but it is not too uncommon to find sentences with a missing direct object. One study of children aged twenty-two to twenty-six months found that direct objects were dropped between 4 and 14 percent of the time in patterns where they should have been used.[14]

Most frequent of all, though, are sentences with missing subjects. Depending on the child and the particular speech sample that is considered, subjects are dropped in early child language somewhere between 30 and 60 percent of the time. This is far more often than direct objects are dropped, as the following data from the early multiword speech of Adam, Eve, and Sarah shows.

Percentage of missing subjects and direct objects[15]

	Adam (%)	Eve (%)	Sarah (%)
Subjects	57	61	43
Objects	8	7	15

Caught in the bottleneck

Why are sentences sometimes incomplete? One theory is that children are forced to drop things because of a processing bottleneck.[16]

The basic idea is that building a complete sentence makes too many demands on beginners – they have to find the right word, combine it with another word, get them in the right order, and then repeat the whole process for the next word. As a result, their circuits get overloaded, and not all words that they intend to say actually make their way into sentences.

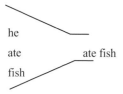

If the processing bottleneck idea is right, words should be dropped more often in long sentences, where the processing demands are greater, than in short ones. Paul Bloom tested this idea by examining the use of subjects in twenty hours of speech produced by Adam, Eve, and Sarah. Just as the processing bottleneck hypothesis predicts, he found that the likelihood of a subject being dropped was greater in longer sentences than in shorter ones.[17]

But why are subjects dropped more often than direct objects? The answer is that children get rid of the most dispensable things first. In many cases, those things just happen to be subjects. For instance, take the second sentence in the following fragment of a conversation.

Where's Mary?
She went home.

It's 100 percent clear who *she* has to refer to here; it must be Mary. A lot of subjects are like this – they tend to refer to someone or something whose identity has already been established.

Because of this, they can be dropped with relatively little chance of misunderstanding, which is presumably why they are often the first thing to go when there's just too much for a young speaker to handle.

5. Missing small pieces

Children's early sentences are frequently missing smaller parts as well – particularly the past tense marker *-ed*, the verb *be*, the possessive marker *-'s*, the plural ending *-s*, the definite article *the*, and the indefinite article *a*.

You can see this by considering the following short excerpts from a transcript made by Harvard researchers of a conversation between Adam and his mother when he was twenty-eight months old. I've filled in the missing items in boldface in the middle column, and I've labeled them in the rightmost column.

What was said	Equivalent adult utterance	Missing pieces
Adam: what dat?	What**'s** that?	contracted form of *is*
Adam: other one.	**the** other one	definite article
Mother: don't touch.		
Adam: touch other one.	touch **the** other one	definite article
Mother: that's very pretty.		
Adam: dat very pretty.	That**'s** very pretty.	contracted form of *is*
Adam: fix screwdriver.	Fix **with the** screwdriver.	preposition; definite article

Mother: you can fix the screws in the firetruck.		
Adam: screw firetruck?	Screw**s in the** fire truck?	plural ending; preposition; definite article
Adam: dat busy bulldozer.	That**'s a** busy bulldozer.	contracted form of *is*; indefinite article
Adam: busy bulldozer truck.	**a** busy bulldozer truck	indefinite article
Mother: how many?		
Adam: two busy bulldozer.	two busy bulldozer**s**	plural ending

Speech that is missing small pieces like these is often called "telegraphic" because of its resemblance to the style of writing used in telegrams and classified ads. (For those who don't remember the days before e-mail, a typical telegram would read something like this: "Arrive tonight 7:00, flight 202.")

When you send a telegram or run a classified ad, you have to pay by the word – so there's a good reason to use as few words as possible. Children in the early stages of language learning also have to "pay by the word" as they struggle to put together their first sentences, and they too see the advantage of communicating as economically as possible.

That doesn't mean that children are totally unaware of endings and "function words" (words such as *the, a, be, with*, and so forth). In one study, an experimenter used two types of sentences to ask children aged twenty-one to twenty-eight months to point to a picture. One type had a definite article in front of a noun ("Find THE dog for me") while the other type put the verb *was* in that position ("Find WAS dog for me").

Even children who were not yet producing *the* in their own speech were better at understanding the first type of sentence than the second.[18] There's also evidence that infants as young as eleven months of age are surprised when *a* or *the* is replaced by a nonsense syllable.[19] Plus they know when it appears in the wrong place, as in *book the* versus *the book*.[20]

Children also seem to have a pretty good idea of what *a* and *the* are used for. Recall the "*zav* experiment" discussed in the preceding chapter – seventeen-month-old children knew that *a zav* was a type of doll whereas *Zav* had to be the name of a particular doll.

One by one

Back in the 1970s, one of the pioneers in child language research, Harvard professor Roger Brown, set out to determine whether the missing small pieces of sentence structure that we've been talking about make their appearance in the same order in the speech of all children. He decided that he would say that an ending or a word had been "acquired" if it appeared in 90 percent or more of the contexts where it was needed in three consecutive recording sessions. (The sessions were held about two weeks apart over a period of many months.)

Working with Adam, Eve, and Sarah, Brown found a striking similarity in the developmental order for endings and function words.

Typical developmental sequence[21]

	Item	Examples
1.	*-ing*	playing
2–3.	*in, on*	in the house, on the bed
4.	plural *–s*	cats, books
5.	irregular past tense	ate, ran
6.	possessive *-'s*	Cromer's car
7.	*is, are*, etc. (uncontractible)	Guess where he is
8.	*the, a*	the apple, a snack
9.	regular past tense (*-ed*)	walked, jumped
10.	the verbal ending *–s*	She knows

Remember though that these are only TENDENCIES. This order is not absolute, and there are often differences from child to child.

What do developmental sequences like these tell us about how children learn language? By keeping track of which suffixes and function words children learn first, it's possible to identify some of the factors that facilitate or impede language acquisition.

Work to date suggests that four of the most important factors are regularity, frequency, phonetic "visibility," and semantic transparency.

Factors enhancing development	Factors impeding development
regular form	irregular forms
frequent occurrence	infrequent occurrence
easy to perceive	hard to perceive
clearcut meaning	subtle or unclear meaning

The suffix -*ing* and the prepositions *in* and *on*, which occupy the first positions in Brown's list, have all four properties. They have no irregular forms, they are relatively frequent, they are full syllables and therefore easy to hear, and they have relatively straightforward meanings.

In contrast, the verbal ending -*s* (as in *He works hard*) is not particularly audible or frequent and lacks any clear-cut meaning. Not surprisingly, it is at the bottom of Brown's list.

A subtler case involves the contrast between the verbal ending -*s* and the -*s* suffix that is used to mark plural nouns (as in *four cars*). Neither -*s* is a full syllable and both are highly regular, but plural -*s* is acquired first. Why?

The key factor in this case may involve frequency, as illustrated in the following data from a sample of parental speech to children.[22]

Relative frequency of two -s suffixes

	all positions combined	end of the sentence
plural -*s*	285	148
verbal -*s*	55	9

Note that plural -*s* occurs far more frequently than verbal -*s*, especially at the ends of sentences (as in *Those are books*) – a position of special salience.

There's still much that we don't understand about developmental order. Why, for instance, are *the* and *a* acquired relatively late? After all, they're regular, relatively audible, and frequent. Could it be something about their meaning that makes them hard to learn?

Probably. These words are notoriously difficult for adult second language learners too, even after they receive intensive instruction and practice. But what makes some meanings more difficult than others? This is something that we simply do not understand well at this point in time.[23]

6. Learning to say "not"

When adults want to deny something (that it's raining outside or that eggplant tastes good), they take the negative word *not* and place it after a "light" verb such as *can*, *be*, *have*, or *do*. (These verbs are called "light" because they don't have much meaning of their own. They are also commonly called "auxiliary" or "helping" verbs because they go along with a regular verb such as *go*, *read*, *eat*, and so forth.)

Statement	Negation
It's raining outside.	It's **not** raining outside.
She has finished.	She has **not** finished.
I may leave.	I may **not** leave.

If a sentence doesn't already contain a light verb, then it cannot be negated unless *do* is added.

Statement	Negation
Eggplant tastes good.	Eggplant **does** not taste good.
I ate my supper.	I **did** not eat my supper.

Children's first negations are different from those of adults in several respects. There's confusion over whether to use *no* or *not*. There's often no light verb for the negative word to combine with. And the negative word sometimes occurs in the wrong place in the sentence.

Is it no *or is it* not?

Children often use *no* rather than *not* as their negative word. This happens in two of the following sentences.[24]

No singing song.
Not have coffee.
Not write this book.
No eating that one.

It's not completely clear why *no* so often replaces *not*.

One possibility is that *not* is harder for children to hear. It is often buried in the middle of the sentence, where it gets contracted to *n't*. (We usually say *I wasn't watching* rather than *I was not watching*.)

In contrast, *no* usually occurs by itself or at the beginning of a sentence (*No, you can't have that*), where it is often stressed (sometimes screamed!). That may make it more evident to children, which would help explain why they latch onto it as a way to negate sentences.

No light verbs

Because children don't have light verbs in their early speech, they have to let the negative combine directly with words of other types.

Child's sentence	Corresponding adult sentence
No singing.	"She is not singing."
No cup.	"That is not a cup."
No ready.	"I'm not ready."

These patterns gradually disappear as verbs such as *be* are acquired and make their way into children's sentences.

A negative beginning

When a sentence contains both a subject and a negative, either of two things can happen. Usually, the negative comes between the subject and the verb, in approximately the same place that it occurs in adult speech.

Me no do that.
Mommy not here.

However, in some cases the negative comes first. Here are some apparent examples from the speech of children between the ages of eighteen and thirty months.[25]

No the sun shining.
No I see truck.
Not Frazer read it.
No Mommy giving baby Sarah milk.
No Mommy doing. David turn.
No lamb have it. No lamb have it.
No lamb have a chair either.
No dog stay in the room. Don't dog stay in the room.
Don't Nina get up.
Never Mommy touch it.
No Leila have a turn.
Not man up here on him head. (= "The man isn't up here on his head.")

There is disagreement over whether these sentences are really what they appear to be. It seems that in at least some of these cases the negative word isn't denying the truth of the sentence at all. Rather, it's a response to something that has just been said. That is, a child who says *No car going there* may mean "No, the car is going there" rather than "The car is not going there."

And at least some of these sentences have an altogether different type of meaning – the *no* at the beginning of the sentence is used to mean something like "I don't want." Consider the following excerpt from a conversation between two-year-old Nina and her mother.[26]

Mother:	Can you put it on the floor?
Nina:	No have it, Mommy.
Mother:	You don't want me to have it?
Nina:	*No. No. No lamb have it. No lamb have it.*
Mother:	You don't want the lamb to have it either.

Notice that the sentence *No lamb have it* means something like "I don't want the lamb to have a chair," not "The lamb doesn't have a chair."

Something similar happens in the next excerpt too.

Mother:	Let me try it. [as mother takes the whistle]
Nina:	Yeah.
Mother:	What's Mommy doing?
Nina:	*No Mommy doing. David turn.* [as Nina brings whistle to David]

It's pretty clear that when Nina says *No Mommy doing*, she means "I don't want Mommy doing it," not "Mommy isn't doing it."

Does this mean that there are no genuine cases of pre-subject negation? There probably are *some*. For example, when my daughter was eighteen months old and we were discussing noise, she proudly proclaimed *No MG noisy. No.*, meaning "Our MG isn't noisy." (An MG is a British roadster.)

But she didn't use this type of pattern often. Like MGs, cases of real pre-subject negation seem to be exceedingly rare. In fact, in Kenneth Drozd's study of 123 children, only 10 produced this sort of pattern even once.[27]

7. *I*, *me*, and *my*

An important feature of English pronouns – words like *I*, *you*, *he*, and *she* – is that they typically change their form depending on whether they are used as a subject, a direct object, or a possessor.

Used as a subject	Used as a direct object	Used as a possessor
I can go.	Mommy saw **me**.	**my** book
You can go.	Mommy saw **you**.	**your** book
He can go.	Mommy saw **him**.	**his** book
She can go.	Mommy saw **her**.	**her** book
They can go.	Mommy saw **them**.	**their** book

For many children, the first step in the acquisition of pronouns is to use – and overuse – the direct object forms (*me, him, her*, etc.). So these forms show up in the direct object position, where they belong, and in the subject position, where they don't.

Direct object forms in the direct object position (where they belong)[28]
Cuddle ME. (21 months)
Help ME out. (20 months)
Pinch HIM. (21 months)
Paula put THEM. (18 months)
Want THEM. (24 months)

Direct object forms in the subject position (where they don't belong)[29]
ME got bean. (17 months)
ME want one. (21 months)
ME sit there. (21 months)
HER do that. (20 months)
HIM gone. (20 months)
HIM naughty. (24 months)

In contrast, subject forms are rarely, if ever, found in direct object positions.[30] So, you probably won't hear a child say *Help I* for *Help me*, or *Watch she* for *Watch her*.

Why do only direct object pronouns tend to be overused? Perhaps because they are more noticeable. Unlike subject pronouns, they can show up alone rather than being always buried inside a sentence. (If I ask "Who's there?," you answer "Me," not "I.")

But there's an interesting additional puzzle that this idea doesn't explain: children are more likely to overuse *her* than other direct object pronouns. When Matthew Rispoli studied pronoun forms in the speech of two- and three-year-olds, he found that *her* replaced *she* almost half the time. In contrast, *him* took the place of *he* and *them* took the place of *they* only about 10 percent of the time.[31]

Error	Frequency (%)
she → her	49
he → him	11
they → them	12

Why does this happen?

Rispoli thinks that the answer may lie in the following table of English pronoun forms.

Subject form	Direct object form	Possessor form
I	me	my
he	him	his
she	**her**	**her**
they	them	their

Notice that *her* shows up twice – once in the direct object column (*I saw her*) and once in the possessor column (*her book*). (Rispoli calls this the "double cell" effect, since *her* occurs in two "cells," or places, in the table.) It is possible that these two uses "gang up" to overwhelm the corresponding subject form in a way that the solitary *me*, *him*, and *them* forms cannot.

It's also possible that the answer lies in the speech that children hear around them. When Carson Schütze examined a one-million-word English text, he found that *I* was about twice as frequent as *me* and *my* put together, while *he* was almost four times as frequent as *him*. In contrast, *she* and *her* occurred with approximately equal frequency,[32] presumably because *her* does double duty as both a direct object pronoun and a possessive pronoun.

If the same is true of the way parents speak when their children are listening, then it may turn out that *I* and *he* are resistant to replacement simply because they occur so much more frequently than the forms that might otherwise invade their space.

Overusing object pronouns is a common error, but not all children do this. Some seem to get the subject and object forms more or less right from the beginning, with error rates of less than 5 percent.[33] And some children take a more roundabout route, going through a stage where the subject form *I* has to compete not only with the object form *me* but also with the possessor form *my*.[34]

I like Anna.
I cried.
MY want the little ones.
MY taked it off.
ME jump.

There's a lot of controversy about just how many children use *my* as a subject and how often they do it. If the reports so far are right, a *my* subject is most likely for actions controlled by the speaker and for emphasis.[35]

MY blew the candles out.
MY cracked the eggs.
MY wear it. [asking to wear a microphone]

8. Who? What? Where?

Words like *who, what, where, why, how,* and *when* are used to ask questions in English. Because of their spelling, they are often called "*wh*-words" and the questions in which they appear are called "*wh*-questions."

Some wh-*questions*
WHERE did Mommy go?
WHAT can I do?
WHO left this on the floor?
WHY do I have to go to bed?

There's a tendency for *where* and *what* to show up first, followed by *who, how,* and *why.* (Don't forget, though, that these are only statistical tendencies; the developmental pattern for any particular child could well be different.)

Developmental order for wh-*words*[36]

Wh-word	average age of acquisition (months)
where, what	26
who	28
how	33
why	35
which, whose, when	after 36 months

There's probably a simple explanation for the early acquisition of *where* and *what*. As many as 80 percent of the *wh*-questions that some parents use contain *where*.[37] And parents often ask more *what* questions than *who* questions, since there are usually more unfamiliar objects than unfamiliar people in the child's environment to ask questions about.

What are you asking about?

The development of question structures is also sensitive to the grammatical function of the *wh*-word, especially whether it corresponds to the sentence's subject or its direct object.

Subject wh-*question*
Who is helping Max? (Answer: *Mary* is helping him.)

Direct object wh *question*
Who is Max helping? (Answer: He is helping *Susie*.)

Karin Stromswold examined subject and object questions in the speech of twelve children, beginning when they were between fourteen and thirty months of age.[38] After looking at about 13,000 *wh*-questions, she concluded that some children started using subject *wh*-questions first and some children asked direct object *wh*-questions first. Overall, though, all children seem to ask more subject *wh*-questions than direct object *wh*-questions.

All other things being equal, we expect direct object *wh*-questions to be harder, since they depart from the normal subject–verb–direct object order of English.

Direct object *wh*-question
Who is Max helping ?
↑
The *wh*-word   Normal position
occurs here, at   for a direct object
the beginning of
the sentence

Possible answer: He's helping SUSIE.

In comparison, subject *wh*-questions should be easy since the subject occurs in its normal position at the beginning of the sentence.

Subject *wh*-question
Who is helping Max?
↑
The subject *wh*-word
is in the normal
position for subjects
Possible answer: MARY is helping him.

Naoko Yoshinaga found a simple way to test this.[39] She sat down with a child and a stuffed animal (Pooh Bear), and then took out a picture like the following.

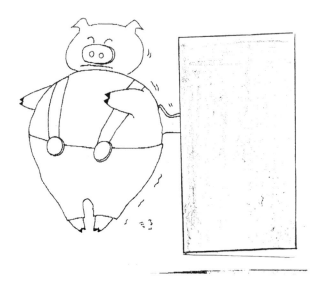

Notice that this picture depicts an action involving two participants, but that one of them is mostly covered up.

The experimenter then said:

Someone is pushing the pig, and Pooh knows who. Can you ask him who?

The right response here is "Who is pushing the pig?" – a subject *wh*-question.

A second type of picture depicted a different situation.

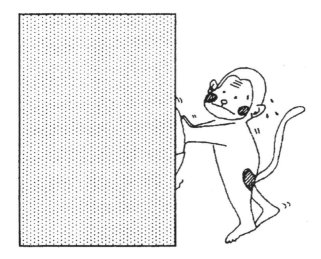

This time the experimenter said:

> The monkey is pushing someone, and Pooh knows who. Can you ask him who?

The correct response here is "Who is the monkey pushing?" – a direct object *wh*-question.

The children got the subject *wh*-questions right almost all of the time, but they had a lot of trouble with direct object *wh*-questions. The two-year-olds got hardly any right, and the three-year-olds succeeded less than half the time.

Results of the question experiment (percent correct)

	Age groups (years)			
Type	2	3	4	Average
subject *who*	100%	97.2%	88.6%	93.5%
dir. obj. *who*	8.3	41.7	79.6	55.4

When the children had trouble with a direct object question, they almost always ended up producing a subject *wh*-question instead.

So, in response to the second picture above, they would say "Who is pushing the monkey?" instead of "Who is the monkey pushing?"

What the child should say:	*What the child actually says:*
Who is the monkey pushing?	Who is pushing the monkey?
dir. obj. subject verb	subject verb dir. obj.

Notice that the end result of this mistake is a sentence in which the subject occurs in its usual position before the verb, and the direct object occurs in its usual position after the verb.

Not all direct object questions are hard, though. Children have little or no trouble with questions such as *What is the monkey drinking?*, for example. That's because they can use and interpret such sentences without paying close attention to the word order. Given the meaning of *drink, what* has to be the direct object and *monkey* has to be the subject – the reverse wouldn't make sense.

The true difficulty of *wh*-questions reveals itself only when experimenters look at sentences such as *Who is the monkey pushing?* and *Who is pushing the monkey?* These sentences can be correctly interpreted only by paying attention to the word order. And that's where children have trouble.

9. *Yes–no* questions

English has a second major type of question, which is called a *yes–no* question because the expected answer is either "yes" or "no."

Are you watching TV?
Can I go now?
Will Mary be there?

Questions of this sort begin with a light verb (*are, can, will,* and so on). Regular "heavy" verbs cannot occur at the beginning of a *yes–no* question: we do not say things like *Read you the book?* or *Went Mary?*

Now, of course, the beginning of a sentence is not the usual place for light verbs in English. Generally, they occur between the subject and the sentence's main verb, as in *I C A N do that*. For this reason, linguists often say that the light verb has to be "moved" to the beginning of the sentence in order to make a question.

statement   *yes–no question*
He can go   ---   *Move the light verb*   -->   Can he _ go?
                                                   ↑_____|

Sometimes things go wrong, though. Children occasionally produce sentences in which they put one light verb at the beginning of the sentence and its twin in the middle of the sentence.[40] (This is called a "copying error.")

Why **did** you **did** scare me? (age 3;2)
Is it**'s** Stan's radio? (age 2;6)

And sometimes they make questions in which the tense shows up twice. (Most errors of this type occur when the light verb is *do*.)[41]

Did you **came** home? (age 1;10–2;6) [should be: Did you come home?]
 ↑   ↑
Past tense Past tense

Does he **makes** it? (age 2;10) [should be: Does he make it?]
 ↑   ↑
Pres. tense Pres. tense

But these are not SYSTEMATIC errors. That is, children don't go through a stage in which all of their *yes–no* questions look like this. Rather, these are errors that they make just sometimes, which suggests that the mental machinery used to build question patterns malfunctions occasionally.

What might cause this malfunction? One possibility is that children simply get distracted by the fact that there are so many things that have to be done at once when building a sentence – choosing the right words, getting them in the right order, pronouncing them intelligibly, and so on.

Thinking along these lines, Mineharu Nakayama reasoned that children should make more errors in relatively complicated questions than in simple ones.[42] But what might make one question more complicated than another?

Long moves

Remember that *yes–no* questions are formed by placing a light verb at the beginning of the sentence and that this verb comes from a position after the subject. It therefore makes sense to think that sentences with longer subjects might be harder than sentences with shorter subjects, since the light verb has farther to travel.

Statement	Question	Distance traveled by light verb
	short subject	
The boy was sleeping	Was **the boy** _ sleeping?	2 words
	long subject	
The boy who fell was skating	Was **the boy who fell** _ skating?	4 words

Nakayama thought of a way to test this by having children respond to requests such as the following.

Ask Pooh Bear if the dog is sleeping on the mat in the hall.
Ask Pooh Bear if the boy who is watching a small cat is happy.

To make the task more realistic, there were pictures like the following that Pooh Bear could consult before giving his answer.

Ask Pooh Bear if the dog is sleeping on the mat in the hall.

Ask Pooh Bear if the boy who is watching a small cat is happy.

In response to the first task, an adult would say

Is the dog sleeping on the mat in the hall?

And in response to the second task, we would say

Is the boy who is watching the small cat happy?

Both questions are equally long – ten words – but they differ in terms of *where* the length is. In the first sentence the subject (*the dog*) is only two words long, but in the second one it is eight words long (*the boy who is watching a small cat*). This means that the light verb has a lot further to "travel" in the second sentence.

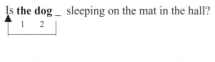

Nakayama found that children were far more likely to make errors in sentences with long subjects. In fact, the proportion of correct scores on these sentences averaged only 44 percent, compared to over 95 percent on some sentences with shorter subjects.

About half of the errors involved saying the light verb twice, once at the beginning of the sentence and once right after the subject.

Is the boy who is watching the small cat **is** happy?

↑

repeated verb

About a quarter of the errors involved stopping partway through the sentence and starting over again, this time using a pronoun subject.

stop & restart

↓

Is the boy who is watching the small cat – **is he** happy?

↑

pronoun subject

Adults do this too, by the way, when they find themselves in over their heads. Long moves are tough for everyone, it seems.

10. Other constructions

We've already seen that there is no limit to how long a sentence can be – another word or phrase can always be added. The key to a sentence's capacity for growth lies in the combinatorial potential of the individual words from which it is made. For example, I can build a sentence that consists of just a noun and a verb.

noun	*verb*
Bobbie	went.

But I can also choose a verb that allows me to add another verb.

noun	*verb*	*verb*
Bobbie	likes	**eating**.

And that other verb might allow another noun.

noun	*verb*	*verb*	*noun*
Bobbie	likes	eating	**popcorn**.

And that noun might allow me to add another entire sentence, and so on.

noun	*verb*	*verb*	*noun*	---------*sentence*---------
Bobbie	likes	eating	popcorn	**that his mother makes**.

Children are quick to figure this out. From the very early stages of multi-word speech, they learn verbs that allow them to build long sentences. In one study of twelve children, for example, the following verbs showed up before age three.[43]

By age two and a half: want, need, like, watch, see, lookit, let, ask, say, make, gonna

By age three: think, tell, guess, know, hope, show, remember, finish, wonder, wish, help, say, pretend, decide, forget

These are the types of verbs that allow a sentence to grow outward, and children take advantage of this pretty quickly.

At first, they just add another verb, or perhaps a pronoun (like *me* or *him*) and a verb.

I wanna **go**.
You gonna **stay**.
Watch **me go**.
Let **me go**.

Before long, entire sentences start to show up after the first verb.[44]

Want **lady open it**. (Daniel, 19 months)
Want **teddy drink**. (Jem, 21 months)
Do it **how I do it**.
I guess **she is sick**.   } age 28 to 30 months
I don't know **who it is**.

A sentence can also be made longer by joining it to another sentence with the help of a connective such as *and, because, but, when*, and so forth.[45]

Maybe you can carry that **and** I can carry this. (Kathryn, 29 months)
They're taking a vacuum cleaner to wipe **and** puppy dog's running. (Eric, 29 months)
I'm going this way to get the groceries **then** come back. (Kathryn, 29 months)
You better look for it **when** you get back home. (Peter, 38 months)
Maybe you can bend him **so** he can sit. (Kathryn, 29 months)
Get them **'cause** I want it. (Eric, 29 months)
I think **that** that's where the baby will go. (Kathryn, 29 months)

These connectives start to show up in children's sentences sometime between age two and two and a half. The first connective to make an appearance is invariably *and*, with *then, when, because, where, but, if, that*, and *so* not far behind.

The arrival of relatives

When children are two and a half years old or so, sentence-like structures start showing up after nouns, as in the following examples. (The technical – and not very helpful – name for this type of sentence is *relative clause*.)

Look at that noise . . . **you're making again**. (age 31 months)
I want something **that the cow(s) eat**. (age 33 months)

Relative clauses are like sentences in that they always contain a verb (notice *make* and *eat*, in the above examples). Their job is to provide information about the noun to their left. So, in the first example, the relative clause *you're making again* helps to identify which noise the speaker is talking about – it's the one that you're making again.

Children don't have that many chances to produce relative clauses in their everyday conversations. That's why studies of relative clauses in child language often have to create situations that call for this sort of structure.

One way to do this is to show children pictures such as the following.[46]

The children are then asked "Which dog is the pig looking at?" The experimenter has her back turned, so the child can't simply point or say "this one." Instead, he has to think of a way to describe the right picture.

Put yourself in the position of the child for a minute. What are you going to say to the experimenter? If you have learned relative clauses, this is exactly the situation in which you would use one. In fact, you'd probably say something like, "The dog who is wearing a hat." (Notice the relative clause, *who is wearing a hat*.)

And sure enough, this is what children do too. Even two- and three-year-olds succeed at producing a relative clause in this sort of situation over 85 percent of the time in some experiments.[47]

Summing up

Sentences are built by combining words into patterns of particular sorts. Some of these patterns are very short and simple (like *Let's go* and *I'm hungry*). Others, like negations, *wh*-questions, *yes–no* questions, and relative clauses, are considerably more complicated.

Learning to build these various types of sentences is one of the major tasks of language learning. Nonetheless, as we've seen in this chapter, it's accomplished with astounding speed – even a three-year-old has a firm grip on the sentence-building tools of his language.

But building sentences is only part of the story. For sentences to do their job of conveying messages, they have to be interpreted and used in particular ways. This is the topic of our next chapter.

5 What sentences mean

In the preceding chapter, we focused on the form of sentences – whether the words are in the right order, whether any parts are missing, whether the right pronoun is used, and so on. But that's only half the story, at best. We also need to think about how sentences convey meaning.

We'll begin by looking at children's early one-word and two-word utterances to see what types of meanings they express and what they tell us about children's early linguistic abilities. We'll then move on to consider a series of more advanced constructions, each of which provides valuable clues about children's emerging abilities to understand and to communicate.

1. What a word can do

From the day they say their first word, children are amazingly good at finding ways to express themselves and at interpreting what adults say to them. Children's first utterances usually consist of just a single word, but it's often used to express a sentence-like meaning.

A child who points to her father and excitedly says "Dada, Dada!" is doing more than naming the person who just entered the room – she's trying to express the meaning "Here's Daddy." And a child who looks at her mother's gloves and says "Mama" is not confusing the gloves with her mother – she's trying to say something like "Those are Mommy's gloves."

Single-word utterances are often called *holophrases* (literally "whole sentences"). Adults use them too – as when we say "butter" for "Pass the butter please" or "Stop" for "Stop yelling in my ear." But for children that's all there is at first. Here are some other examples of holophrases and of the types of meaning that they commonly express.

Some examples of one-word utterances[1]

utterance and context	likely interpretation	age (months)
dada, looking at father	Here's daddy.	8
nana, in response to mother's "no"	I want to do that.	11
dada, offering bottle to father	You take this.	11
ball, having just thrown ball	I'm throwing the ball.	13
Daddy, hearing father approach	Daddy is coming.	13
up, reaching up and in answer to "Do you want to get up?"	I want to get up.	13
down, having just thrown something down	I'm throwing it down.	14
caca ("cookie"), pointing to door of room where cookies are kept	The cookies are in there.	14
box, putting crayon in box	The crayon goes in the box.	15
fishy, pointing to empty fish tank	The fish isn't there.	15
again, when he wants someone to do something again	Do it again.	18

It's not easy for a child to express all that she wants to say in single-word sentences. It requires a lot of ingenuity to be that economical, and children seem to follow a very sensible policy – they tend to pick a word that expresses what is new or changing or uncertain about the situation.

That's why a child trying to get down from a chair will say *down* rather than *me* or *chair*. She's describing the change that she wants to have happen. (Patricia Greenfield and her colleagues, who have studied one-word utterances in great detail, call this the *Informativeness Principle*.[2])

The Informativeness Principle fits well with a basic fact about the human perceptual system – our attention tends to focus on what is novel, changing, and uncertain in the world around us.[3] Which leads us to expect that parents too will be guided by this principle when they use one-word utterances in speaking to their children.

This seems to be right. A study of Hebrew-speaking children and their mothers revealed that 97 percent of the children's one-word utterances looked like one-word sentences that had occurred in their mothers' speech.[4]

How much can children understand in the one-word stage?

Parents often feel that young children can understand far more than they can say, especially during the one-word stage. But what does the evidence show?

The simplest and most successful technique for studying this question takes advantage of the fact that children have a natural tendency to look at situations that match what they are hearing.[5]

Here's how a typical experiment is set up. As in the technique used to investigate early word comprehension (chapter 3, section 2), the child sits facing two TV monitors. Once her attention has been drawn to a light directly between the two monitors, she hears (for example) the sentence *She's kissing the keys*. At the same time, the TV monitors in front of her are depicting two scenes – one showing a woman kissing keys while holding a ball and the other showing a woman kissing a ball while holding a set of keys.[6]

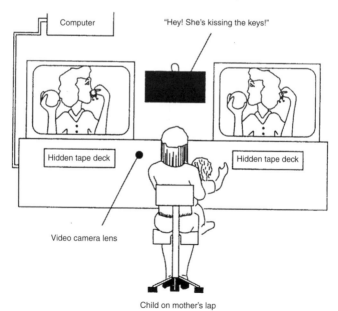

Child on mother's lap

If infants understand the sentence, they should prefer the screen depicting the woman kissing the keys. If, on the other hand, the infants are just hearing the individual words without connecting their meanings, they should pay equal attention to both screens since each depicts a kissing action as well as a set of keys.

The experimenters measured the amount of time it took for children to decide which monitor to look at and the amount of time they spent watching it. The children's performance was not perfect (sometimes they focused on the wrong TV screen), but they did demonstrate a preference for the screen that matched what they heard – they tended to look at it more quickly and to watch it longer.

So one-year-old children really do seem to be able to understand more than they can say. Of course, that doesn't mean that they can understand EVERYTHING that adults can understand or even that they go about understanding things in the same way that adults do. We'll come back to this point in a little while. First, though, let's have a look at the types of meanings that children express once they start building two-word sentences.

2. Two is better than one

Having a second word in an utterance makes a big difference. Children can say a lot more, and the chances of it being understood are much higher. Here are some sample two-word utterances from children's speech, along with a brief description of their meaning.[7]

Sentence	Meaning that is being expressed
Eve read.	doer + action
Hit ball.	action + undergoer
Daddy cookie.	doer + undergoer (= "Daddy eat cookie.")
Daddy shoe.	possessor + thing (= "Daddy's shoe")
Big train.	property + thing
Book table.	thing + location (= "The book is on the table.")
Come here.	action + location
That book.	naming (= "That's a book.")
More cookie.	recurrence (= "There are more cookies.")
No milk.	nonexistence (= "There is no milk.")

Children differ from each other quite a bit in terms of which two-word patterns they use most. Some children prefer doer + action patterns; others use more action + undergoer sentences. Possessor + thing patterns are relatively common, while doer + undergoer sentences tend not to be.

How much can children understand in the two-word stage?

As we saw a little earlier, preferential looking experiments suggest that very young children are able to interpret complete sentences (such as *She's kissing the keys*). What is not clear from that experiment is precisely HOW the children are doing it.

One thing that makes sentences such as *She's kissing the keys* relatively easy to understand is that the relationships among the parts are not reversible. That is, it's possible for a woman to kiss keys, but it's not possible for keys to kiss a woman.

What happens when children in the one- and two-word stage try to interpret reversible sentences like *Cookie Monster is tickling Big Bird*? In preferential looking experiments, even children aged sixteen to nineteen months can respond correctly more often than not.[8]

But they also make a lot of mistakes, both in this type of experiment and in other sorts of experiments as well. For example, when they are asked to use toys to act out the meaning of sentences like *The truck bumped the car*, children often respond by making the car bump the truck.[9]

Evidently, children know the meaning of *bump*, but they have difficulty keeping track of who does the bumping (the "doer" or subject) and who gets bumped (the "undergoer" or direct object). They aren't yet skilled at using a sentence's word order to figure out its meaning.

How word order makes a sentence interpretable

The **truck**   bumped   the **car**.
1st noun   2nd noun
  ↓   ↓
doer/subject   undergoer/direct object

Even after children start to do well on reversible sentences in act-out experiments (usually around the age of three, give or take a few months), we can still ask whether their success is due to "big rules" or "little rules." (Remember from the preceding chapter that a big rule applies to all verbs, while a little rule applies to just one verb.) That is, when a child reaches the point where she can understand *The truck bumped the car*, is it because she has figured out that the subject/doer routinely precedes the verb and that the direct object/undergoer follows it (a "big rule")? Or has she just learned that things work this way for *bump* (a "little rule")?

In order to answer that question, experimenters taught two- and three-year-old children novel verbs by showing them funny actions (like one toy animal pushing another one down into a chute) and then saying "Do you see that? That's called BLICKING."[10]

Once the children had learned the new word, they were asked to "Make Cookie Monster blick Big Bird." If they knew the big rule, they would realize that Cookie Monster has to be the doer and Big Bird the undergoer. On the other hand, if they were learning a little rule for each verb, they'd have trouble knowing who does what to whom.

In general, children younger than age three do not do very well on this sort of task. They get some right just by guessing, but scores in the 80 percent range often don't show up until children are three and a half or even older. This result is very similar to the outcome of the experiment we looked at in the preceding chapter, in which children had to *produce* their own sentences rather than just try to understand someone else's.

So, it looks like children learn to speak and understand in roughly the same way: at least for word order, they start out with little rules. It then takes some time (perhaps a year or so) before they discover and get used to the big rule that associates the subject/doer with the position before the verb and the direct object/undergoer with the position after the verb.

Ironically, as we'll see in the next section, the big rule causes problems of its own in certain types of sentences.

3. Passive sentences

Although the subject of an English sentence usually names the doer, things don't always work this way. In so-called "passive" sentences such as the one below, the subject names the undergoer.

The car was bumped (by the truck).
　　↑
　subject
　(undergoer)

Two other features of passives are also evident in this sentence: they always include a light verb such as *be* or *get*, and the doer is either not mentioned or is accompanied by the preposition *by*.

The car was bumped (by the truck).
　　　↑　　　　　　　　↑
　light verb　　　　doer
　　　　　　　(does not have to be mentioned)

Children's early passives sentences

Children usually start producing passive sentences when they are three years old. More often than not, the doer is not mentioned in these sentences.

Some passives from the speech of Adam[11]
So it can't BE CLEANED? (3;2)
I don't want the bird to GET EATED. (3;7)
I want to BE SHOOTED. (3;8)
Why he gon' BE LOCKED in a cage? (3;10)
Mommy, de cow gonna GET LOCKED UP. (4;0)

Some passives from the speech of Christy and Eva[12]
Do you think that flower's supposed to BE PICKED by somebody? (Eva, 2;10)
She brought her inside so she won't GET ALL STINKED UP by the skunk. (Eva, 4;1)
I just GOT PINCHED from these pointed stuff. (Eva, 3;3)
Does the cream of wheat need to BE COOLED? (Eva, 4;2)
Hair needs to BE BRUSHED. (Christy, 4;2)

Not only do three- and four-year-old children produce passive sentences, they often go one better than adults by over-producing them. Here are a few examples of children's passive sentences that no adult would ever utter.[13]

> Is it all NEEDLED? (3;2)
> It WAS BANDAIDED. (3;4)
> . . . they won't GET STALED. (3;6)
> The tiger will come and eat David and then he will BE DIED . . . (4)
> I want these pancakes to BE SUGARED. (4;2)
> Why IS the laundry place STAYED open all night? (4;3)
> How WAS it SHOELACED? (4;4)

Children are also very good at catching the subtle difference in meaning between passives that use the light verb *be* and those that use *get*. Adults tend to use the *get*-passive mostly for actions that have negative consequences (e.g., **I** *just* **got** *bitten by a mosquito*) and the *be*-passive for situations with more neutral consequences.

Nancy Budwig took a careful look at passive patterns in the speech transcripts of two children over a period of several years, beginning when they were two years old.[14] She found that they systematically made the same contrast between *be* and *get* that adults do.

Why passives are still hard to understand

Despite all of this, something very strange happens when children are given comprehension tests – they often can't understand passives!

A typical comprehension test works something like this. The child sits at a table with the experimenter, and the experimenter reads her a series of sentences one at a time. As she hears each sentence, the child is shown two pictures and has to point to the one that the sentence describes.[15] For instance, the experiment might say "The dog is bitten by the cat," and have the child select one of the pictures below.[16] (Another commonly used comprehension test involves giving the child a set of toys and asking her to act out the meaning of the test sentences.)[17]

Children under age five usually do very poorly on these tests, typically getting less than 50 percent of the passive sentences right. In contrast, they do very well on "active" sentences such as *The cat bit the dog*, in which the subject is the doer.

Most children do better on certain types of passive sentences than on others. For example, even children who misinterpret sentences like *The dog was bitten by the cat* often do well on the following passive sentences.

> The carrot is eaten by the rabbit.
> The pencil is dropped by the girl.

That's because sentences like these two can be understood without paying attention to whether they are active or passive. When you have a carrot and a rabbit and the verb *eat*, there's really only one thing that can happen – the rabbit has to eat the carrot, since carrots can't eat rabbits.

But things aren't so easy in all passive sentences. In the case of the sentence *The dog was bitten by the cat*, you can't tell what happened just by thinking about dogs and cats – in real life, either one could bite the other. So it's necessary to adopt another strategy. For young children, that other strategy often involves a matter of numbers.

Most sentences involving a doer and an undergoer are active, with the subject naming the doer and the direct object naming the undergoer. In fact, probably fewer than 5 percent of the sentences that children hear are passives.[18]

So it's natural for children to expect the sentences that experimenters give them to be active too. This expectation is sometimes referred to as the *Canonical Sentence Strategy*.[19]

The Canonical Sentence Strategy
Expect the first noun to be the doer and the second noun to be the undergoer.

It's easy to overturn this expectation if the passive sentence has no sensible "active" meaning. That's why children have no trouble interpreting a sentence like *The carrot was eaten by the rabbit*, where it just wouldn't make sense to think of the first noun as the doer.

But things aren't so easy with a sentence like *The dog was bitten by the cat*, since there's nothing nonsensical about a dog biting a cat or vice versa. The only way to interpret this sentence correctly is to notice the little words *was* and *by*, and the suffix *-en*.

And that's where the problem seems to lie. These items are just not that audible, since they are both short and unstressed. Often, they go unnoticed by children in the rush to interpret the sentence, and the Canonical Sentence Strategy takes over.

What the Canonical Sentence Strategy does:
The dog was bitten by the cat.

    ↑   ↑
[1st noun = doer   2nd noun = undergoer]
→ the meaning "The dog bites the cat."

The effects of the Canonical Sentence Strategy are strongest in three-year olds, who may succumb to it 80 percent of the time or more. (That is, they correctly interpret passives only about

20 percent of the time.) Older preschool children do somewhat better, with scores on passive sentences typically ranging from 30 to 70 percent correct (compared to over 90 percent correct on active sentences).

So, children *are* capable of understanding passive sentences at least some of the time. Which is hardly surprising, since they can produce them in their own speech. It just seems to take a while to get good at noticing the clues that mark someone else's sentence as passive.

4. Understanding things that aren't there

In the previous chapter I made the point that sentences are like trees whose branches can sprout outward in many different directions. For example, if a sentence contains the verb *know*, it can expand outward by permitting the addition of another entire sentence.

We know.
We know [children eventually grow up].

The bracketed sequence of words in this example is a complete, self-contained sentence. Sometimes, though, a partial or incomplete sentence can appear in that position. For example, the second part of the following sentences consists of a verb and a direct object, but no subject. (To help make this clear, I've put in a dot to represent the missing subject.)

<pre>
                verb   dir. obj.
                 ↓   ↓
The plumber tried [. to fix the leak].
The boy hopes [. to paint the house this summer].
The children wanted [. to see that movie].
The bank decided [. to approve the loan].
</pre>

The subject of the second verb in these sentences is "understood," to use the informal term. That is, it is not explicitly stated, but its identity can be easily figured out. We know that the person fixing the leak is the plumber, that the person who'll paint the house is the boy, and so forth. Let's use a two-headed arrow to help keep track of this information.

The plumber tried [. to fix the leak].
↑_____↑

The boy hopes [. to paint the house this summer].
↑_____↑

Keeping it short

Things get a bit more complicated, though. The following sentence is a case in point.

Mom told Paul [. to wash the dishes].
↑
understood subject

Here there are two nouns to the left of the understood subject (*Mom* and *Paul*).

If you're a speaker of English, you know that the second one is the missing subject of *wash*. (That is, Paul – not Mom – is supposed to wash the dishes.) The "rule" is probably something like this.[20]

The Minimal Distance Principle
To find a missing subject, look for the nearest previous noun.

This works in the "*tell* sentence" above, where there are two previous nouns.

nearest previous
noun
↓
Mom told Paul [. to wash the dishes].
↑___↑

And, of course, it works in sentences where there is only one previous noun, which is therefore automatically the "nearest" one.

```
nearest previous
     noun
      ↓
The plumber tried [ . to fix the leak].
      ↑_____↑
```

So far, so good. But there's a famous pattern for which the Minimal Distance Principle doesn't work.

Making promises

The problem lies in the particular type of "promise" sentence exemplified below. (Readers who grew up in North America will probably find this sentence natural, but I'm told that *promise* cannot be used in this way in British English.)

Dad promised Paul [. to wash the dishes].

The Minimal Distance Principle tells us that the understood subject of *wash* should be *Paul*, but this isn't right. It's Dad, not Paul, who is going to do the dishes.

```
           the nearest previous noun
                    ↓
Dad promised  Paul [ . to wash the dishes].
 ↑_____↑
```
The right meaning: Dad is going to wash the dishes.

One of the most famous child language experiments ever deals with just such sentences.

In the late 1960s, Carol Chomsky conducted an experiment on "*promise* sentences" as part of the research she was doing for her doctoral dissertation at Harvard.[21] Sitting at a table with a child (she studied forty children in all, aged five to ten), she first made sure that the child understood what the verb *promise* meant. Here are two sample excerpts from that part of the experiment. (I've written the children's responses in small capitals to make them easier to spot.)

SCOTTY (age 5)
What do you do when you promise someone something?
WHEN YOU DON'T FOOL.

JIMMY (age 6;10)
You're walking home from school with your friend, and as you're saying good-bye you promise him that you'll call him up this afternoon. How would you say that?
I'LL CALL YOU RIGHT UP AFTER LUNCH.

With that out of the way, Chomsky then asked the child to act out the meaning of various *tell* and *promise* sentences with the help of toys.

Bozo tells Donald [. to hop up and down]. Make him do it.
Bozo promises Donald [. to hop up and down]. Make him do it.

All the children did fine on the *tell* sentences – they'd make Donald hop up and down. (Remember that *tell* sentences obey the Minimal Distance Principle.)

```
          nearest previous
               noun
                ↓
Bozo tells Donald [ . to hop up and down].
             ↑_____↑
```

But the younger children had trouble with the *promise* sentences. Instead of making Bozo hop up and down (the adult interpretation), they once again made Donald hop.

```
   the children's interpretation
                ____
             ↓     ↓
Bozo promises Donald [ . to hop up and down].
  ↑_____↑
   the adult interpretation
```

You can probably see what's going on here – the children hadn't figured out that *promise* is an exception to the Minimal Distance

Principle. They therefore interpreted the nearest previous noun as the understood subject of *hop*.

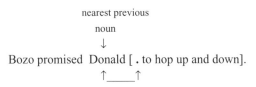

It's easy to see

Carol Chomsky's dissertation included one other famous experiment. It involved the following sentence, in which the second verb (*see*) has both an understood subject and an understood direct object. (I'll use a dash to indicate the understood direct object.)

The doll is easy [. to see _].

Although this sentence is only six words long, it reveals just how complicated language can get. The Minimal Distance Principle picks the doll as the subject of *see* – that is, as the one who sees. (Remember that when there is only one preceding noun, the Minimal Distance Principle automatically picks it as the missing subject.)

The doll is easy [. to see _].
   ↑_____↑

But that's wrong. The right interpretation is something like "It is easy to see the doll," in which the doll is interpreted as direct object of *see* (the thing that is seen), and no particular person is identified as its subject.

The doll is easy [. to see _].
 ↑_____↑

Do children know this?

Chomsky's experiment in this case was extremely simple: she showed the child a blindfolded doll and asked, "Is the doll easy to see?"

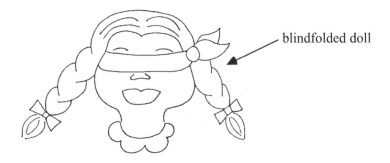

blindfolded doll

Is the doll easy to see?

An adult would interpret this sentence to mean "Is it easy to see the doll?" (with *the doll* as direct object of *see*). And since the doll is in plain sight, the right answer is "yes."

Quite a few of the children in Chomsky's experiment did answer correctly, as the following excerpts from their conversations with her show.

A N N C. (age 8;8)
Can you tell me, is the dolly easy to see or hard to see?
    EASY.
Could you make her hard to see? Can you think of a way?
    IN THE DARK.

A N N M. (age 8;7)
Is the doll easy to see or hard to see?
    EASY.
Would you make her hard to see?
    SO YOU CAN'T SEE HER AT ALL?
Okay.
    (Child places the doll under the table.)
Tell what you did.
    I PUT HER UNDER THE TABLE.

However, more than a third of the children responded incorrectly. Here are some examples of the types of things they said.

ERIC (age 5;2)
Is the doll easy to see or hard to see?
> HARD TO SEE.

Will you make her easy to see?
> OKAY. [He removes blindfold.]

Will you explain what you did?
> TOOK OFF THIS. [pointing to blindfold]

And why did that make her easier to see?
> SO SHE CAN SEE.

LISA (age 6;5)
Is the doll easy to see or hard to see?
> HARD TO SEE.

Will you make her easy to see?
> IF I CAN GET THIS UNTIED.

Will you explain why she was hard to see?
> [to doll:] BECAUSE YOU HAD A BLINDFOLD OVER YOUR EYES.

It's clear from these conversations that some of the children thought they were being asked about whether it was easy for the doll to see things. Because the doll was blindfolded and therefore couldn't see anything, they answered "no."

But why would they think that the question meant this in the first place? Possibly they were using the Minimal Distance Principle to figure out the identity of the understood subject rather than the identity of the understood direct object. This then gave them the incorrect interpretation depicted below, in which they identified the doll as the subject of *see*.

The doll is easy [. to see _].
     ↑_____↑

5. Understanding pronouns

Pronouns are energy-saving devices that allow us to refer to someone or something whose identity we already know without using a name (like *Bob*) or an article + noun combination (like *the man*).

> **Bob** thinks that **he** can go. (he = Bob)
> **The man's** own dog bit **him**. (him = the man)

Even very young children seem to know the function of pronouns, since they are eager to use them if a preceding noun has already established what they refer to. There's a very simple way to see this.

When children are asked to imitate a sentence, they often make changes so that it sounds the way THEY think it should. This tendency yields a very interesting result when children aged two and a half to three and a half are asked to repeat a sentence like the following, in which the same noun occurs twice.[22]

> Because **Sam** was thirsty, **Sam** drank some soda.

They often replace the SECOND noun by a pronoun, saying something like:

> Because Sam was thirsty, **he** drank some soda.

And when they're given a sentence in which the pronoun comes before the noun, they often change it so that the pronoun comes after the noun.

> Because **he** was thirsty, **Sam** drank some soda.
> $\Downarrow$
> Because **Sam** was thirsty, **he** drank some soda.

Evidently, even very young children have figured out that pronouns are used to refer to someone who has been recently mentioned. That's the easy part.

Reflexive responses

One of the things that makes the acquisition of pronouns challenging is a contrast between "plain pronouns" such as *he/him* or *she/her* and "reflexive pronouns" such as *himself* or *herself*.

Plain pronouns	Reflexive pronouns
I/me	myself
you	yourself
he/him	himself
she/her	herself
it	itself
we/us	ourselves
they/them	themselves

One difference between the two types of pronouns shows up in patterns where one sentence occurs inside a still larger sentence. In the examples that follow, I've put brackets around both the main sentence and the smaller sentence that's inside it, and I've marked each sentence with an "S" subscript.

_____main sentence_____
[$_S$ Mandy thinks [$_S$ *Suzie pinched someone*]].
　　　　　　　smaller sentence inside

Now look at what happens when we use a pronoun in place of *someone*.

[$_S$ Mandy thinks [$_S$ Suzie pinched herself]].
[$_S$ Mandy thinks [$_S$ Suzie pinched her]].

If I say *herself*, the person who got pinched has to be Suzie. On the other hand, if I say *her*, it's either Mandy or it's someone not mentioned in the sentence. But it can't be Suzie.

The rules that we follow here can be stated as follows. (Of course, I'm simplifying this a bit, but that doesn't matter for what we want to do next.)

The Reflexive Pronoun Rule
Reflexive pronouns must refer to someone mentioned in the same small sentence.

The Plain Pronoun Rule
Plain pronouns cannot refer to someone mentioned in the same small sentence.

The Reflexive Pronoun Rule tells us that *herself* refers to Suzie, since she is mentioned in the same small sentence (the one inside the inner brackets).

[s Mandy thinks [s Suzie pinched herself]].

The reflexive pronoun refers to a noun in the same small sentence.

And the Plain Pronoun Rule tells us that *her* cannot refer to Suzie in this type of sentence, although nothing prevents it from referring to Mandy.

[s Mandy thinks [s Suzie pinched her]].

The plain pronoun does not refer to a noun in the same small sentence.

There are various ways to figure out when children learn to make this distinction. One technique involves asking them to act out the meaning of sentences with the help of dolls and other toys. For example, an experimenter might take a Mickey Mouse doll and a Donald Duck doll and say:

> Donald thinks that Mickey Mouse scratched himself. Show me what Mickey did.

or

> Donald thinks that Mickey Mouse scratched him. Show me what Mickey did.

If the child correctly understands the first sentence, she'll have Mickey scratch Mickey. If she understands the second one, she'll have Mickey scratch Donald.

Another way to study the interpretation of pronouns is to ask children questions about pictures. Here's an example from an actual experiment.[23]

Here's a picture of Mama Bear and Goldilocks

Is Mama Bear touching her? [Yes]   *Is Mama Bear touching her?* [No]

A child who understands how plain pronouns work will answer "yes" for the first picture and "no" for the second one. In contrast, if the question is *Is Mama Bear touching herself?*, the correct answer is "no" for the first picture and "yes" for the second one.

Regardless of how the experiment is done, the results with children aged three to five are pretty much the same.[24] Even the younger children tend to do very well with the reflexive pronouns. But they have trouble with plain pronouns, which they tend to interpret as if they were reflexives. So, they often say that yes, Mama Bear is touching her when looking at the picture on the right.

Why do children make mistakes on plain pronouns? One possibility is that reflexive pronouns are easier to interpret because you don't have to look as far to find out who they refer to. (Because of the Reflexive Pronoun Principle, the person they refer to has to be mentioned in the same small sentence.)

Children seem to adopt a similar effort-saving strategy when they interpret a plain pronoun too. They look to see if there is someone mentioned in the same small sentence to whom it might refer. And when there is someone, the children sometimes decide to look no farther – they simply let the pronoun refer to that person.

[s Mama Bear touched her].
↑_____↑

Despite their problem interpreting some plain pronouns, children appear to make almost no mistakes when it comes to choosing between plain pronouns and reflexive pronouns in their own speech.

In one painstaking study, researchers examined about 100,000 utterances produced over a three-year period, beginning when the children were two years old.[25] They found that both *me* and *myself* were used correctly at least 95 percent of the time, with only occasional mistakes.

> Mistake involving *me*: I see **me**. (Adam, 34 months, looking through a telescope)
> Mistake involving *myself*: Don't you drop me . . . you hurt **myself**. (Abe, 34 months)

So it seems that children actually know the distinction between plain and reflexive pronouns at a very early age. They just have trouble using it under some circumstances. As you may recall, something similar happens with passive sentences, which children produce in their own speech but sometimes have trouble understanding in the speech of others.

This sort of phenomenon has led many linguists to distinguish between linguistic competence (*knowledge* of language) and linguistic performance (the ability to *use* that knowledge in particular circumstances – including contrived experiments where unfamiliar people are showing you funny pictures and asking strange questions).

It is widely recognized that children's competence far exceeds their performance in most cases, which is why researchers are constantly looking for techniques that will allow a more accurate assessment of what children know and when they know it.

6. Pronouns and stories

All of the above notwithstanding, children do have at least one problem with plain pronouns. As the following example from a talkative two-year-old helps show, children who are telling a story often use pronouns in ways that make it difficult to know who they are referring to.[26]

Researcher:	Can you tell me about the barbecue that you had?
Child:	We had a barbecue right over here and I told him to don't put it . . . I told Dan what he was doing. And . . .
Researcher:	You told Dan what he was doing?
Child:	Yeah. And when I was doing it I turned, pushed him, what I do pushed way up high.
Researcher:	You pushed him way up high.
Child:	Yes. But he turned to go.
Researcher:	But he what?
Child:	He turned to go on me. He didn't come to my house.

Even the researchers who recorded this story were baffled.

> What in the world is the child talking about here? In the above example, she states that she "told him to don't put it." Yet who is being told? "The Dan of the next sentence or someone else?" And who is Dan? He is nowhere identified, and could be a peer or a parent of another child or some other adult. Is the "he" in the next sentence also Dan? What is being put? And what is the child doing when she "was doing it?" Who is the "him" she turned and pushed?

In another study, four-year-olds who were asked to describe pictures frequently used pronouns in ways that made them difficult to interpret. How, for example, could anyone be expected to know that the first *she* in the following story refers to a girl and the second *she* to a woman?

> . . . she's sitting on the seat airplane . . . she's giving something to a girl, now she's looking at a book . . . now she's putting the thing up high.

The ambiguous use of pronouns is very common (and totally normal) in the speech of preschool children. It is noticeably less frequent among six- and eight-year-olds, whose sensitivity to the perspective and informational needs of others has improved with time and experience. In fact, older children will sometimes even stop in mid-sentence to correct an unclear use of a pronoun.[27]

> . . . and she's lea . . . and the girl is leaning . . .

Strange stories

Pronouns are not the only thing that children have trouble keeping track of when telling stories. Many of their early stories are also missing important contextual information about the participants, the place where the event took place, and its time. The following example is from two-and-a-half-year-old Todd.[28]

Todd:	I gonna bring this. (a tape recorder)
Researcher:	Where are you gonna bring it?
Todd:	Out here.
Researcher:	Okay.
Todd:	He bite my leg.
Researcher:	What?
Todd:	Duck bite my leg.
Researcher:	The dog bit your leg. Oh, oh, the duck. Oh boy!
Todd:	Me go in the water.
Researcher:	You went in the water.
Todd:	Yeah. My leg.
Researcher:	You were telling me about a duck?
Todd:	He bites. (screaming)
Researcher:	He bites.
Todd:	And kick.
Researcher:	And kick.
Todd:	Duck bite me and kick me and duck kick me and, and bite.

Notice that Todd provides no information about where he was, when the events happened, or who was with him. This sort of information often has to be coaxed out of children by their parents. In fact, in doing this, parents may well be giving their children an idea of the type of "scaffolding" that a story requires. Notice how much more detailed three-and-a-half-year-old Cathy's story is, with its explicit information about the participants and the time and place of the key event.[29]

Researcher:	Have you ever gotten stung by a bee?
Cathy:	But Ian [her brother] got a big sting when he was first born.
Researcher:	Ian had a big sting when he was first born?
Cathy:	Yeah.
Researcher:	Well, tell me about it. What happened?

Cathy: I was walking with him and, and I just and he falled and
            he didn't know that he falled right on a bee. And he, and
            his knee was on a bee and stung, he got stung on a bee.

This is perhaps not an epic tale, but it does contain the rudiments of truly informative communication, which is what learning a language is all about.

7. Can you quantify that?

If someone tells you that John read a book last night, you'd know right away that a single book was read. But the interpretation of *a* is not always so straightforward, as you can see by considering the following sentence.

> EVERYONE read A BOOK last night.

We can use this sentence to describe a situation in which Jerry, Lou-Ann, and Sandy all read the same book. Or we can use it to describe a situation in which there are three different books: it's possible that Jerry read *Charlotte's Web*, Lou-Ann read *Old Yeller*, and Sandy read *The Mark of Zorro*. That's because *a* can interact with *everyone* semantically, so that there can be as many books as there are readers.

This type of interaction is very common when two quantifiers (words such as *every* and *a*, which express quantities) occur in the same sentence, especially when the word denoting the larger quantity (e.g., *every*) is part of the subject and the word denoting the smaller quantity (e.g., *a*) is part of the direct object. There are many other examples of this.

> All the children wanted to see a movie.
> Each gift comes in a box.
> Many of the culprits attend one of the schools in this neighborhood.
> Most students are interested in something.

How good are children at understanding sentences containing quantifiers? Remarkably good, it seems. An impressive piece of evidence for this comes from a question-and-answer experiment in which children are shown a picture and then asked a simple question.

For example, in order to determine whether children understand the interaction between *every* and *a*, experimenters show them pictures like the ones below and ask them, "Is every child riding a horse?"[30]

"Is every child riding a horse?"

Even three-year-olds respond "yes" for both pictures, demonstrating that they understand that *a* can be interpreted on its own (giving the meaning "one and only one") or can interact with *every*.[31]

However, children do sometimes have trouble with the interaction between *every* and *a*. The problem shows up when they are shown a picture such as the following, and are asked "Is every girl riding an elephant?"[32]

"Is every girl riding an elephant?"

Children sometimes respond "no" to this question, explaining that there is one elephant who is not being ridden![33] They seem to think that the sentence should describe a symmetrical situation in which there is an elephant for every girl and a girl on every elephant.

There is clearly something very difficult about this picture – in fact, even adults are sometimes taken aback by it. But why do children apparently misinterpret it in the way that they do?

One idea is that the meaning of *every* can somehow "spread" through the sentence for children. As a result, it applies both to girls and to elephants, giving a meaning like "Every girl is riding an elephant and every elephant is being ridden by a girl."[34]

Another idea is that the question is misleading without a proper context. Normally, we don't ask a question when the answer is obvious – as it is here. We'd be more likely to ask whether every girl is riding an elephant in a situation where there is some doubt as to whether this has actually happened.

In a new series of experiments, children aged three to five were presented with a story in which a mother talks with her two daughters about whether they should drink soda or hot apple cider after skiing (note the two possible outcomes – having soda or having cider).

After expressing an initial preference for soda, the girls are persuaded to follow their mother's example and have apple cider. Reinforcing the possibility of an alternative outcome, the picture accompanying the story depicts five cups of apple cider A N D five bottles of soda.[35]

When asked whether every skier drank a cup of apple cider, the children overwhelmingly responded in the affirmative. Not a single child responded negatively on the grounds that two of the five cups of cider were untouched. (However, two children did remark that they thought "every skier" was too strong a statement to make when there were just three skiers in the story!) Once again, it seems that children may know more than can be revealed in a single experiment.

Summing up

Overall, the picture that emerges from the study of how children learn the meaning of sentences is a familiar one. No matter how complicated things get, it all seems to come naturally to children.

From their first attempts at one- and two-word speech, they are skilled at expressing themselves with the limited means at their disposal. Their ability to understand the speech of others is even more advanced, running well ahead of their expressive abilities.

Children make relatively few comprehension mistakes. And the few errors that do occur reveal much about how they learn to interpret sentences. Initially, it seems, children rely on small word-based rules ("the noun to the left of *read* refers to the doer, the noun to the right refers to the undergoer"). Later, bigger generalizations (like the Canonical Sentence Strategy and the Minimal Distance Principle) emerge, dramatically increasing the child's interpretive powers.

Sometimes, as we have seen, these generalizations are TOO powerful. But the occasional mistakes they yield are manageable and disappear in time, as children become better at dealing with exceptions and special cases.

So far in this book, we've talked about words, sentences, and their meaning, but we've said nothing about pronunciation. The next chapter looks at how children come to perceive and produce the sounds of language.

6 Talking the talk

The first sound that a child makes is a shrill cry as air enters his lungs at birth. Cooing noises begin around the age of two or three months. The production of speech-like sounds under the guise of babbling begins at about the same time or a little afterward and is usually fully developed by the age of six months or so. The child's first real words often start to show up around the age of ten or twelve months.

Age range	Typical sounds[1]
birth to one month	crying, burps, grunts
two to three months	cooing
four to six months	squealing, yelling, growling, trills made with the lips, marginal babbling
seven to twelve months	full-fledged babbling
ten to eighteen months	first words

Long before a child tries to say anything, though, he listens. How children perceive speech is also a good place to begin thinking about how they come to learn the sound system of their language.

1. An ear for language

Children seem to be especially designed to listen to language. In fact, they don't even wait until they are born to start. Speech can be heard in the womb – not clearly enough to discern individual sounds, but with enough clarity to make out the intonational contour and other features of the speaker's voice. But how can we know whether this prenatal experience has an impact?

Because infants exhibit an inborn tendency to turn their heads toward the source of a sound, it is possible to identify their early listening preferences by keeping track of when they turn their head and how long they look.[2] It's even possible, with the help of an electronic pacifier, to teach them to select the type of auditory stimulation they prefer (for example, a tape of one language versus another).[3]

These techniques have led to a number of important findings. For instance, newborns prefer their mother's voice to other female voices.[4] They prefer the language of their parents over other languages.[5] And they are able to recognize that an English sentence does not sound the same as a French sentence, for example.[6]

But it doesn't stop here. In one study, mothers-to-be read aloud a story every day during the last six weeks of pregnancy.[7] Two days after birth, their infants were tested to see whether they found the story more soothing than an unfamiliar story. And indeed they did – even when the story was read by someone other than their mother. Evidently they had been able to pick up enough of the story's rhythm while in the womb to recognize it after they were born.

That study is trumped by another experiment in which mothers-to-be recited a children's rhyme out loud every day over a four-week period.[8] The familiar rhyme (but not an unfamiliar one) was found to bring about a decrease in heart rate in 37-week-old fetuses – further evidence that children are sensitive to the sound pattern of language even before they are born.

Consonants in the cradle

Prenatal speech perception is apparently limited to general rhythmic and intonational features of language, so there are still many details left to learn after birth. Foremost among these is the language's inventory of consonants and vowels.

Here again, work with very young infants calls for special techniques. We know that an infant's heart rate and sucking rate change when he is exposed to a new type of stimulus. (Special equipment – including an electronic nipple – makes it possible to measure these things.)

So, in order to find out whether an infant can hear the difference between "b" and "p," experimenters play a series of "b" sounds over a period of several minutes, followed by a "p" sound (. . . *ba ba ba ba pa*). If there is change in heart rate or sucking rate right after the *pa* is introduced, we know that he notices the difference between "b" and "p."[9]

Infants aged one to four months are able to hear the difference between pairs of consonants. By the time they are six months old, they can hear the differences among vowel sounds as well.[10]

Infants are even able to distinguish between sounds in languages other than the one they hear at home. In one experiment, six- to eight-month-old infants who were being raised in English-speaking homes could hear contrasts among consonants in Hindi and Nthlakampx (a Native Indian language spoken on the west coast of Washington state and British Colombia). By the time children are ten to twelve months old, though, they are already beginning to have difficulty hearing distinctions not found in their own language,[11] which seems to have become their primary focus.[12]

By the way, infants aren't the only ones who are gifted at hearing the difference among speech sounds. Various type of animals have shown similar abilities, including chinchillas, macaques, and even quail.[13] This suggests that at least some of the perceptual mechanisms relevant for speech have their roots deep in the mammalian auditory system and beyond.

2. Can you hear that?

By the time a child is a year old, he has begun to learn the words of his language. At this point, sounds are not just sounds anymore – they are pieces of words. And listening involves using those sounds to hear and identify words. This is quite different – and harder – than just noticing that two sounds are not quite the same.[14] Nonetheless, children do remarkably well from a very early age.

A simple technique for studying children's ability to distinguish among words was developed by the Russian linguist N. Shvachkin in the 1940s. It involves showing children pairs of pictures whose names differ by just one sound. (Such words are called *minimal pairs*.)

In some variants of this method, the names are made-up words like *bok* and *pok* (Shvachkin himself did it this way). In other studies, real words are used (e.g., *seat* and *feet*)[15] or a combination of real words and made-up words (like *car* and *gar*).[16]

Using Shvachkin's method, we can determine whether a child can hear the difference between "k" and "g" by showing him the following pair of pictures and saying "Show me the coat" (or "Show me the goat").

If he points to the right object, we have an indication that he can hear the difference between the "k" and "g" sounds. (Of course, the test has to be done more than once to make sure that he didn't get the right answer just by guessing.)

When techniques like these are employed, the results show that children can use phonetic differences to distinguish among words long before they are able to make the distinctions in their own speech.[17] Indeed, some studies report that by age two or earlier, children can distinguish among words almost as well as adults can.[18]

I said "fis," not "fis"

Being able to HEAR a sound is not the same thing as being able to MAKE it, of course. And there is ample evidence that children have trouble pronouncing many of the phonetic contrasts that they are able to perceive. Here's just one example.

> One of us . . . spoke to a child who called his inflated plastic fish a *fis*. In imitation of the child's pronunciation, the observer said: "This is your *fis?*" "No," said the child, "my *fis*." He continued to reject the adult's imitation until he was told, "That is your fish." "Yes," he said, "my fis."[19]

Notice how the child rejects the experimenter's imitation of his "fis" pronunciation. It's obvious that he is able to hear the difference between "s" and "sh" in adult speech even though he can't yet make it himself.[20]

Do children perhaps make phonetic distinctions in their own speech that adults cannot hear? Could it be that the "*fis* boy" has two "s" sounds in his speech – one for words like *fish* and the other for words like *miss* – and that he can hear the difference between them even though adults can't?

Something like this does sometimes happen. In the course of learning the contrast between "t" and "d," for instance, at least some children go through a stage where they have two different "d" sounds, one of which is a bit more like "t" than the other.[21] Adults can't hear the difference, but it is picked up by the machines that phoneticians use to analyze speech.

In general, though, children aren't very good at hearing subtle distinctions in their own pronunciation. For instance, when three-year-olds listen to tape recordings of their own speech and of adult speech, they can interpret only about 50 percent of their own pronunciations – compared to nearly 100 percent of the adult pronunciations.[22]

How do you spell that?

An intriguing indication of children's sensitivity to speech sounds comes from an unexpected source – their early attempts at spelling. Preschool children who have learned the alphabet but have not yet been taught to spell in the conventional way sometimes engage in spontaneous attempts to write. The result is a natural system of "phonetic transcription" that reveals just how aware children are of the way language is pronounced.[23]

Take words such as *pencil*, *open*, and *kitten*, for instance. If you listen carefully to your normal "fast-speech" pronunciation of these words, you'll notice that the second syllable doesn't contain a vowel. It consists just of the "l" or "n" consonant. Children's invented spellings reflect this – they frequently write PESL for "pencil," OPN for "open," and KITN for "kitten."

Or take the pronunciation of the "t" sound when it occurs between vowels, as in *pretty*, *letter*, and *bottom*. In North American speech, the "t" is pronounced as a sort of rapidly articulated "d." (Linguists call this sound a "flapped D.") Children pick up on this too, which is why we find spellings like PREDE for "pretty," LADR for "letter," and BODOM for "bottom."

Children are also aware of the fact that the English past tense ending has three separate pronunciations, depending on the preceding sound. For example, it's "t" in *laughed*, "d" in *stayed*, and "id" in *waited*. Which is why children write LAFFT for "laughed," STAD for "stayed," and WATID for "waited."

Children's ability to perceive the subtleties of pronunciation is indeed impressive, but it's only half of what it takes to learn the sound system of language. Articulation – being able to actually pronounce the sounds – is the other (and harder) half. We'll turn to that next.

3. Babbling

Children show an interest in how speech sounds are produced before they can make any themselves.

Infants aged ten to sixteen weeks old prefer to watch the image of a speaker whose lip movements are in synchrony with his speech to one whose lip movements are accompanied by a voice delay of a half second.[24] Evidently, they realize that mouth movements are responsible for sounds and expect to see the two coordinated with each other.

The first sign of speech-like sounds in children comes when they begin to babble, typically at around four to six months of age. Most early babbling consists of repeated (or "reduplicated") syllables such as *dada*, *mama*, *baba*, and the like. As we saw in chapter 2, with a little parental imagination and encouragement, some of these forms eventually take on a meaning and become the child's first words.

Babbling increases in frequency and complexity until the age of about twelve months.[25] It may overlap with the production of real words for several weeks before eventually dying out.

Nonetheless, babbling doesn't seem to be crucial for the later development of real speech. Children who are unable to babble (because they have to breathe through a tube in their throat during the babbling stage) subsequently acquire normal pronunciation.[26] Moreover, even deaf children babble, although not as much or as fluently as children with normal hearing.[27]

Babbling across languages

Babbling is not easy to study. Children's early sounds are often poorly articulated and run together with each other. (Part of the problem is that an infant's speech organs are quite different from an adult's – everything is smaller, the voice box is higher in the throat, there are no teeth, and the palate is not as high.[28]) Nevertheless, some good progress has been made in understanding its basic properties.

It was once thought that babbling children produced all the possible sounds of human language.[29] But that's just a myth. In fact, in most cases, children produce far fewer sounds than are found even in their own language – let alone all the languages of the world. (That doesn't mean that they can't hear the difference between speech sounds from other languages; we're talking about speech production now, not perception.)

There's quite a bit of similarity among children the world over in terms of the sounds that are most likely to show up during babbling. One study of fifteen languages (including English, Thai, Japanese, Arabic, Hindi, and Mayan) uncovered the following tendencies among babbling children.

Common and uncommon sounds during the babbling phase[30]

Frequently found consonants	Infrequently found consonants		
p b m	f	v	th
t d n	sh	ch	j
k g	l	r	ng
s h			
w y			

Are babbling children influenced at all by the language they hear around them? They must be, since their babbling bears some resemblance to the language being learned, especially in its intonation.

In one experiment, samples of babbling from children learning French, Arabic, and Cantonese were presented to adult speakers of French, who were asked to pick out the children learning that language.[31] The adults were able to make the right choices about three-quarters of the time for six-month-old infants, apparently by paying attention to the intonational melody of their babbling.

Another feature of babbling is even subtler, but every bit as fascinating. Two researchers did an analysis of children learning English, French, Japanese, and Swedish, taping their speech at four different times – when they had no words at all and then when they had a vocabulary of four words, of fifteen words, and of twenty-five words.

They found that the proportion of various sounds in children's babbling is very similar to the proportion of those same sounds in adult speech. For example, if we look at the relative frequency of sounds produced by the lips ("p," "b," "m," "f," and "v") in adult speech, it turns out that French uses these sounds more than English and that English uses them more than either Swedish or Japanese.

These differences are reflected in the way children babble. French infants produce a higher percentage of these sounds in their babbling than do American infants. And American infants produce more than Swedish or Japanese infants.[32] In these respects at least, the children are just like their parents.

4. Early vowels and consonants

From around age thirteen or fourteen months, give or take a few months in either direction, children start producing recognizable words. There are basically two ways to track their ability to produce sounds during this period.

One is to record and transcribe children's spontaneous speech in ordinary situations (play, meals, and so on). The other is to elicit speech from them, usually by playing a naming game with pictures such as the following.[33] (It's also possible simply to have the child repeat words that are said by the experimenter,[34] but the naming technique may give a more accurate idea of what he can do on his own.)

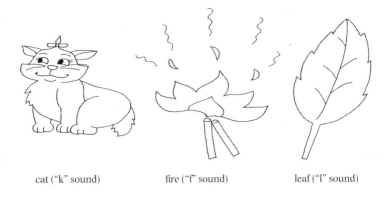

cat ("k" sound)   fire ("f" sound)   leaf ("l" sound)

It's not easy to study children's early pronunciation. Some children do not articulate their words clearly, and it is not uncommon for a child to be inconsistent in his pronunciation of particular words. In the space of just a few weeks, for example, one child used the following pronunciations for the word *the*.[35]

duh, deh, tuh, zuh, luh, dl, dee, the

Differences in the pronunciation of the same word can occur even within the space of seconds.[36] Nonetheless, there are a few general tendencies to report, with the important caveat that these are just tendencies and that there is considerable variation from child to child.

Early vowels and consonants

Five vowel sounds are typically acquired quite early – "ee," "ah," "oo," "oh," and "uh."[37] These vowels are found in words such as the following. (When linguists discuss sounds, they usually do so with the help of special symbols from the International Phonetic Alphabet. In order to keep things as simple and straightforward as possible, I'll avoid that practice here. However, you can find these symbols and a description of the sounds they represent in Appendix 2 at the end of the book.)

bee ("ee")
top ("ah")
moo ("oo")
low ("oh")
nut ("uh")

The most common early consonants in word-initial position are "b," "d," "m," "n," and "h."[38] By age two, a typical English-speaking child can produce the following consonant sounds.[39]

Typical consonant inventory at age two

p	b	m	f	w
t	d	n	s	
k	g			

There's a fascinating correlation between these tendencies and the distribution of particular sounds in the world's languages – the sounds that are acquired early are generally found in more languages than the sounds that are acquired late. Certain sounds are evidently more basic and easier for the human vocal tract to produce.

Even the easy consonants are more likely to be heard at the beginning of a syllable than at the end. As we'll see shortly, children often delete consonants at the end of a syllable, pronouncing *gum* as "guh" and *nose* as "no." The consonants most likely to be pronounced at that end of a syllable in children's early words are "p," "t," "k," and "n."[40]

By age four, the child's inventory of sounds has grown considerably. All the vowel sounds have usually been acquired by this time, as have the consonant sounds listed below.[41] (I've used boldface to indicate the sounds that are likely to have been added after age two.)

Typical consonant inventory at age four

p	b	m	f	**v**	**ch**	**j**	w	**y**
t	d	n	s	**z**			**l**	**r**
k	g	**ng**	**sh**					

Still to be acquired at this age are the "th" sounds in words like *thing* and *that*.

5. Making adjustments

This brings us to the question of what children do when they try to say a word containing sounds that they can't yet pronounce. Sometimes, they avoid saying the word altogether.[42] But more often they either drop the tough sound (deletion) or replace it by an easier one (substitution).

This can happen A LOT: more than 90 percent of the early words produced by some children show the effects of deletion and/or substitution.[43] Let's look at some concrete examples. (If you have a young child at home, you'll probably be able to add dozens of additional examples of your own.)

Deletion

Word-final consonants are prime candidates for deletion, especially in a child's early speech. Initial consonants, in contrast, are typically retained, especially if they come right in front of a vowel.

```
dog → "dah"     bus →"buh"     boot → "boo"
   ↑               ↑               ↑
 delete          delete          delete
```

Deletion in these cases creates a syllable that consists of a single consonant followed by a single vowel. (Linguists call this a "CV Syllable.")

```
CVC     CV
dog →  "dah"
   ↑
 delete
```

CV patterns are initially favored by children the world over, regardless of what language they are learning. They are also the syllable type most widely found in human language in general.

Deletion is also very common when two or more consonants occur in a row within the same syllable. As the following examples indicate, regular rules determine which consonant goes and which one stays.

- When a consonant at the beginning of a word is followed by an "l" or "r," drop the "l" or "r."

    blanket → "banket" or "bankie"
    try → "tie"
    crumb → "kum" or "gum"
    bring → "bing"
    from → "fum"
    sleep → "seep"

- When a nasal consonant ("m," "n," or "ng") is followed by a "p," "t," or "k" at the end of a word, delete the nasal.

    bump → "bup"
    tent → "tet" or "det"

• When an "s" is followed by another consonant, drop the "s."

  stop → "top"
  small → "mah"
  desk → "dek"

You may notice another strategy for some words in which an "s" precedes another consonant – their order is changed.

  ask → "aks"
  spaghetti → "pas-ghetti"

This is a less drastic solution to the phonetic hardship created by "sk" and "sp," since it keeps both consonants. But it still makes things better for the child, since an "s" is easier to pronounce at the end of a syllable than at the beginning if it's next to another consonant.

Substitution

Consonants that survive the deletion process aren't necessarily given an adult-like pronunciation. If they are among the sounds that children have difficulty making, there's a good chance that they'll be replaced by an easier sound. Once again, their fate is determined by fairly regular processes.

• *The stopping process*: Replace a consonant that is produced with a continuous flow of air (e.g., "s," "z," "sh," or "th") by a consonant that is produced by completely cutting off the flow of air (e.g., "t" or "d").

Word	Child's pronunciation	Substitution
sing	"**t**ing"	s → t
see	"**t**ee"	s → t
zebra	"**d**ebra"	z → d
thing	"**t**ing"	th → t
thi**s**	"**d**it"	th → d, s → t
shoe**s**	"**t**oo**d**"	sh → t, z → d

(You can verify for yourself whether a particular consonant is produced with a continuous flow of air by attempting to prolong its pronunciation. You'll notice that consonants such as "s," "z," "sh," and "th" can be prolonged indefinitely, but that consonants such as "t" and "d" cannot.)

- *The gliding process*: Replace "l" or "r" by "y" or "w."

Word	Child's pronunciation	Substitution
lion	"**y**ine"	l → y
laughing	"**y**affing"	l → y
look	"**w**ook"	l → w
rock	"**w**ock"	r → w
sto**r**y	"sto**w**y"	r → w

- *The denasalization process*: Replace a nasal sound ("m" or "n") by a non-nasal sound ("b" or "d").

Word	Child's pronunciation	Substitution
ja**m**	"da**b**"	m → b
roo**m**	"woo**b**"	m → b
spoo**n**	"boo**d**"	n → d

- *The fronting process*: Replace a consonant by a sound that is made more toward the front of the mouth.

Word	Child's pronunciation	Substitution
thumb	"**f**um"	th → f
ship	"**s**ip"	sh → s
jump	"**dz**ump"	j → dz
chalk	"**ts**alk"	ch → ts
go	"**d**oe"	g → d

The figure below summarizes where various consonant sounds are produced in the mouth, starting at the lips. (For further details and a diagram of the vocal tract, see Appendix 2.)

Front				*Back*
Lips	Front teeth	Alveolar ridge (behind the front teeth)	Hard palate	Soft palate
p, b, m	th	t, d, n	sh, ch, j	k, g, ng
f, v		s, z		

Assimilation

There's at least one more important type of sound change in children's speech. You can think of it as a type of substitution, since it involves one sound being replaced by another.

However, unlike the substitutions we've talked about so far, the outcome is determined by a neighboring sound. Put simply, a sound tries to become more like its neighbor in some respect. (Linguists refer to this as *assimilation*.)

One very common type of assimilation involves a sound being modified so that it is produced at the same place in the mouth as its neighbor. A good example of this occurs in words like *impatient*, where the "n" of the prefix *in-* (compare *in*active, *in*direct, etc.) is changed to "m" because of the following "p." (Like "p," "m" is made with the lips; "n" is made with the tip of the tongue.)

$$\textit{"n" becomes "m" to make it more like "p"} \quad \Downarrow \quad \begin{array}{c} \textbf{in} + \textbf{p}\text{ossible} \\ \nearrow \\ \textbf{m} \end{array}$$

Assimilation not only makes words easier to pronounce by reducing the number of differences among neighboring sounds, it is apparently attractive to the ear as well. Infants as young as four months of age prefer to listen to nonsense words such as *umber* compared to *unber*.[44] What's the difference? *Umber* shows the effects of assimilation, since "m" and "b" are both pronounced with the lips.

Another common type of assimilation involves vocal-cord vibrations (or *voicing*, to use the technical term). The vocal cords vibrate during the pronunciation of all vowel sounds, as you can see for yourself if you place a finger on your neck as you say "ee," "ah," or "oh." Some consonants ("z" and "v," for instance) have accompanying vocal-cord vibrations, while others (like "s" and "f") do not.

When a consonant that shouldn't have vocal-cord vibrations occurs in front of a vowel in children's early speech, it often ends up "catching" the vocal-cord vibrations from the vowel. That is, it becomes "voiced," turning into an entirely different sound.

The table below contains some consonant contrasts that are based on vocal-cord vibrations (see Appendix 2 for additional information).

No vocal-cord vibrations	Vocal-cord vibrations
p	b
t	d
k	g
f	v
s	z

In the first two examples below, a "p" picks up the vocal-cord vibrations from the following vowel and turns into a "b." A similar sort of thing happens when "t" turns into "d" (the third example), and "s" turns into "z" (the final example).

Word	Child's pronunciation	Change
pig	"**b**ig"	p → b
push	"**b**ush"	p → b
tell	"**d**ell"	t → d
soup	"**z**oop"	s → z

Sometimes, we even find total assimilation, which makes a sound identical to a nearby sound. The results of this type of change can be seen in the following words.

Word	Pronunciation	Change
doggy	"**g**oggy"	d → g, because of the nearby "g"
self	"**f**elf"	s → f, because of the nearby "f"
Kathleen	"Ka**k**leen"	th → k, because of the nearby "k"
baby	"b**ee**bee"	a → ee, because of the nearby "ee" (written as *y*)

6. Stress is good

One of the most noticeable features of children's early speech is that they often drop entire syllables, especially when they try to pronounce longer words.

Adult word	Child's word[45]
giraffe	faff
mustache	tass
goodnight	na
away	way

This creates a shorter word that is easier to pronounce, of course, but we need to know why children delete the first syllable in these examples rather than the second one. (Children don't pronounce *giraffe* as "gi" or *mustache* as "mus.") The explanation for this seems to lie in the way children perceive longer words.

Take the word *away*, for example. If you pronounce it to yourself, you'll notice that the second syllable (the "way" part) is pronounced more forcefully than the first. This is what linguists call "stress."

English distinguishes three levels of stress – primary stress, secondary stress, and unstressed. A syllable with primary stress is pronounced louder than any other syllable in the word, and its vowel is fully articulated.

In contrast, an unstressed syllable is far less audible, with a short and weak vowel that linguists call a "schwa." The first syllable of a word like *about* and the last syllable of *sofa* contain a weak vowel of this type.

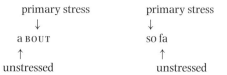

Intermediate between a syllable with primary stress and an unstressed syllable are syllables with secondary stress. They are not pronounced as strongly as syllables with primary stress, but they don't have a weak vowel either.

The second syllable in the words *slowly* and *veto* has secondary stress. In a word like *alligator*, the first syllable has primary stress, the third syllable has secondary stress, and the second and fourth syllables are unstressed. Let's use a double underline for primary stress and a single underline for secondary stress.

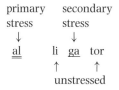

Under the spotlight

Now you can probably guess what's going on in our earlier examples. Because syllables bearing primary stress are more audible than their unstressed counterparts, children tend to zero in on them when they are first learning to speak (remember the "spotlights" discussed in chapter 2). For this reason, the stressed syllable is usually not dropped.[46]

In extreme cases, the stressed syllable may be the only part of the word that is pronounced, even in words containing three or more syllables. (Remember that a double underline marks primary stress and a single underline indicates secondary stress.)

Word	Child's pronunciation[47]
hip po pot a mus	pahs
kan ga roo	woo
spa ghet ti	ge

Sometimes, though, children pronounce only the syllable with secondary stress, especially if it's closer to the end of the word than the syllable with primary stress.

Word	Child's pronunciation[48]
al li ga tor	gay
ca ter pil lar	pi
te le phone	fo

And sometimes, syllables with either primary or secondary stress are spared, but unstressed syllables are dropped.[49]

Word	Child's pronunciation[50]
al li ga tor	agay
a qua ri um	quarium
hel i cop ter	alkat

It's as if children adopted a "Hear no schwas" policy. Unstressed syllables with weak vowels are often just not audible enough to make it past the threshold of perceptibility when a child is getting started on English.

There is one exception to this though – children often keep the *final* syllable of a word, even when it's unstressed. This is probably because the ends of words are easier to notice and remember since they're the last thing a child hears.

Word	Child's pronunciation[51]
ba na na	ana
com pu ter	puter
el e phant	elfun
a ni mal	amul
al li ga tor	gayda

However, even when an unstressed syllable is pronounced, it's often missing one or more sounds. You can see that in the pronunciation of the last syllable of *elephant*, which is missing the "t."[52]

Some children use a completely different strategy for dealing with long words. They produce the same number of syllables that are found in the adult word, but usually only one of the syllables (often the one with primary stress) sounds anything like a part of the adult word.

Twenty-month-old Joshua was like this. In the examples that follow, I've used boldface to mark the syllables in Joshua's pronunciation that seem to be based on syllables in the corresponding adult word.

Word	Joshua's pronunciation[53]
bun ny	**ba** bi
clo ver	**do** do
ti ger	**ta** da
bull do zer	**boo duh** duh
kan ga roo	da da **wu**
mi cro phone	**ma** wuh wuh
vi o lin	wa wa **wi**
straw ber ries	**dah bee** buh

Notice that Joshua's words all have the same "profile" or "silhouette" as the adult words, since the number of syllables is the same. But generally only the stressed syllable resembles the corresponding part of the adult word.

Summing up

Children come into the world already able both to recognize the language of their parents and to make distinctions among the sounds of any language. By age two they have figured out which sounds their own language uses, and they are well on their way to being able to pronounce those sounds themselves. Pronunciation problems – and there are a few, as we have seen – are dealt with in systematic and predictable ways by judicious deletions and substitutions that allow the child to get by until full fluency arrives.

The study of how children come to perceive and pronounce speech sounds, like the study of every other aspect of language acquisition, raises the question that has puzzled researchers for decades – how do they do it? We'll take a closer look at this question in the next and final chapter of this book.

7 How do they do it?

Children are born into a world full of noises and sounds of all sorts (music, car engines, slamming doors, whistling, coughing, crying, conversation, and so on). Somehow, they have to take the part that is speech, break it down into its smaller parts (words, prefixes, suffixes, etc.), determine what they mean, and figure out how to reassemble them in new ways.

Doing this involves mastering a system of sounds, words, structure and meaning whose intricacy typically defeats even the most gifted adult learners. Yet children get the job done before they learn to tie their shoes. How do they do it?

There's still no real solution to this puzzle, although bits and pieces of the answer are starting to emerge. And as this happens, it's becoming clear that certain widely held ideas about how language learning works are probably dead-ends.

The job of this chapter is to try to sort out the difference between the ideas that make sense and those that don't. We'll start by looking at the popular idea that children learn language by imitating their parents.

1. Why it's not imitation

Ask the average person how a child learns language and you'll probably be told "by imitating adults." On the face of it, that makes a lot of sense. The adults in a child's life speak a particular language, and the child ends up speaking that language too.

Imitation of some sort probably is involved in certain aspects of language acquisition. Take words, for example. There's only one way for children to learn that the word for "cat" is *cat* or that the word for "light" is *light*. They have to notice what adults say and then try to do the same thing themselves – in other words, they have to imitate what they hear.[1] It is certainly no accident that humans, the only species with language, have a capacity for vocal imitation that far exceeds anything in monkeys and apes – contrary to popular misconception.[2]

But the imitation explanation won't take us very far. That's because there are major parts of language that cannot be imitated. Sentences are the most obvious example.

Unlike words, which are memorized and stored in the brain, sentences are created as the need arises. You've probably never seen a single one of the sentences in the preceding two paragraphs before in your life, and you'll probably never see any of them again. Yet you understood them, and you could have produced them yourself if you'd been writing this book.

Apart from greetings and other formulaic expressions, many of the sentences we utter and hear every day are novel in this way. They simply don't involve the sort of remembering and repeating associated with imitation.

Two facts about language acquisition confirm that imitation is not the explanation for how children learn to produce sentences.

First, children aren't very good at imitating sentences containing unfamiliar words and structures. They typically repeat only what they can already say. If they've already learned definite articles, they'll repeat a definite article. If they've already learned plural endings, they'll repeat a plural ending. If they've already learned the verb *be*, they'll repeat it. Otherwise, they'll imitate *The dogs are hungry* as *Dog hungry*. Indeed, it is precisely for this reason that experimenters commonly use imitation tests as a way of assessing children's language development.[3]

Second, perhaps because they know they're not very good at it, children don't even try to imitate sentences very often. The proof of this is straightforward – simply take a typical conversation between a mother and her child and calculate how many of the child's utterances are imitations.

The following conversation took place when Adam was two years and eight months old. (The symbol # marks a pause.) You can count a sentence as an imitation if it includes the same "content" words (nouns, verbs, and adjectives) used in the same order as in the utterance just produced by an adult.

1.	Mother:	Do you know what this is?
2.	Adam:	What this is # car.
3.	Mother:	No # that's not a car.
4.	Adam:	Pin.
5.	Mother:	Pin?
6.	Adam:	Yeah # Mommy # pin.
7.	Mother:	What kind of pen?
8.	Adam:	Car.
9.	Mother:	Car?
10.	Adam:	Yeah.
11.	Mother:	What kind of car?
12.	Adam:	Red car.
13.	Mother:	Red car?
14.	Adam:	Yellow car.
15.	Mother:	Yellow car?
16.	Mother:	What do you do with it?
17.	Adam:	[inaudible] watch.
18.	Adam:	Where horses go?
19.	Mother:	Where what go?
20.	Adam:	Where horses?
21.	Mother:	Horse?
22.	Adam:	Horse # go yes Mommy.
23.	Mother:	Did he go to the corral?
24.	Adam:	Did he?
25.	Adam:	There he is # Mommy.
26.	Adam:	Corral corral.
27.	Adam:	Baby horses.
28.	Adam:	Horses.
29.	Adam:	Baby horses.
30.	Adam:	Ready me go?
31.	Adam:	Ready me.
32.	Adam:	Go down dere.
33.	Adam:	Go down right side.

How many times did Adam imitate what his mother had just said during this conversation? He seemed to try just once – in line 2, where he repeats the last part of his mother's sentence (*what this is*). Not a single one of Adam's other sentences contains the same set of content words as a preceding utterance by his mother. In fact, if anyone seems to be imitating, it's Adam's mother – on four occasions (lines 5, 9, 13, and 15) she repeats what HE has just said!

Children vary a great deal in terms of precisely how much they imitate their parents' speech. One study of the speech of six children who were just beginning to produce multi-word sentences found that the proportion of imitated utterances over several taping sessions ranged from around 5 percent in one child to around 40 percent in another.[4]

If anything, this study probably overestimated the extent of imitation in children's speech. That's because the researchers counted an utterance as an imitation even if it was missing a lot of the words that were in the corresponding adult sentence. Here's an example from the speech of twenty-one-month-old Peter, with "imitations" in boldface.

PETER: Open. Open. Open
ADULT: Did you open the tape recorder?
PETER: **Open it**.
ADULT: Did you open the tape recorder?
PETER: **Tape recorder**

It's probably unfair to refer to Peter's "Open it" as an imitation; it's most likely just the answer to the adult's question.

In sum, although children do sometimes repeat what they have just heard (as do adults), imitation does not seem to be a very large part of the picture, especially when it comes to figuring out how sentences work. The key to understanding how children learn language clearly lies elsewhere.

2. Why it's not teaching

If children don't learn language by imitation, then how do they do it? Could it be that parents somehow teach their children to speak by explaining things to them or by correcting them when they make a mistake? That too is unlikely.

Once we go beyond the most superficial things, there's not much that the average person (or even the above-average person) can say about how language works. That's because most of what we know about language is SUBCONSCIOUS: we know it, but we don't know that we know it – and we're therefore not able to explain it to anyone else.

Take the way we use definite and indefinite articles, for instance. Why do we say *I went to school* but not *I went to movie?* If the so-called "definite" article *the* indicates definiteness, then why can it be used in sentences like *The fox is a nocturnal animal* to mean "foxes in general?" Why do we say *the Pacific Ocean* but not *the Lake Michigan?* And why do we usually say *The ball hit him on the arm?* rather than *The ball hit him on an arm?*, even when we're not sure which arm it is?

You know that your mother didn't teach you these things, and you know that you're not going to teach them to your child either.

Then, what about the possibility that parents train their children in roughly the way that one trains a pet? That is, they correct their children when they make a mistake, but they don't try to explain why it was a mistake. There are two big problems with that idea.

For one thing, parents don't try to correct their children's language all that often. When Roger Brown and Camille Hanlon looked at this issue, they found that parents seemed in general to pay little attention to HOW their children said things, although they did seem to care about WHAT their children said.[5] They would respond "Uh huh" to linguistic atrocities like *Her curl my hair*, while correcting perfectly natural sentences like *There's an animal farmhouse* because it was actually a lighthouse.[6]

The other problem with the correction hypothesis is that children often don't respond very well to corrections. Here are a few examples that have been collected over the years.

Example 1[7]

> Child: Nobody don't like me.
> Mother: No, say "nobody likes me."
> Child: Nobody don't like me.
>   [eight repetitions of this dialogue]
> Mother: No, now listen carefully; say "nobody likes me."
> Child: Oh! Nobody don't likes me.

Example 2[8]

> Child: My teacher holded the baby rabbits and we patted them.
> Adult: Did you say your teacher held the baby rabbits?
> Child: Yes.

Adult: What did you say she did?
Child: She holded the baby rabbits and we patted them.
Adult: Did you say she held them tightly?
Child: No, she holded them loosely.

Example 3[9]

Child: Want other one spoon, daddy.
Father: You mean, you want the other spoon.
Child: Yes, I want other one spoon, please Daddy.
Father: Can you say "the other spoon?"
Child: Other . . . one . . . spoon.
Father: Say "other."
Child: Other.
Father: Spoon.
Child: Spoon.
Father: Other spoon.
Child: Other . . . spoon. Now give me other one spoon?

In sum, instruction is neither frequent enough nor effective enough to have a major impact on language learning.

Setting a good example

A related hypothesis is a bit more promising. The key idea is that although parents usually don't make a deliberate effort to correct their children's speech, they often end up providing alternative sentences against which children can measure their own immature utterances.

It's easy to imagine situations in which this could happen: a child says "The dog runned really fast, Daddy" and, without really thinking about it, her father says "Yeah, he ran really fast, didn't he?"

Notice that the father said *ran* where the child said *runned*. He didn't actually try to correct his daughter – in fact, he was probably just trying to agree with her and keep the conversation going – but he did nonetheless set a good example for her.

Linguists call these sorts of responses *recasts*. Here are some additional examples, with the recasts in small capitals to make them easier to pick out.

Some recasts by Eve's mother when Eve was 18 to 27 months old[10]

Eve's utterance	Her mother's recast
It fall.	It FELL?
I don't read no books.	I know you're not going to read ANY books.
A butter.	You want SOME butter?
Have two cracker.	How many CRACKERS?
Man up there.	THERE'S A man up there.
Up wall.	ON THE wall, yeah.
Papa buy some.	Papa BOUGHT some for us.
Faster faster as me.	FAST as me?
Well, what you go do?	What am I GONNA do?
Cromer has he glasses on.	Oh, he does have HIS glasses on.
That's why J. comed.	Yes, J. CAME yesterday, yesterday afternoon.
It doing dancing.	IT's dancing, yes.
That napkins.	Yeah, THEY'RE napkins.
Where's the pencils?	Where'RE the pencils?
Where is them?	THEY're at home.
What I do it?	What DID you do to it?
Cold it.	I know IT's COLD.

In order to get a sense of how recasts fit into an actual conversation, take a look at the following speech sample involving thirty-one-month-old Adam and his mother. I've used boldfaced type for the parts of the mother's recasts that might provide a model that Adam could use to evaluate his incomplete or incorrect utterances. (The # symbol marks a pause.)

1.	Adam:	I got a pant on.
2.	Mother:	You'**ve** got what on?
3.	Adam:	Shoes on # pant on too # shirt on too.
4.	Mother:	Shoes on # **pants** on # shirt on?
5.	Adam:	Yeah.
6.	Mother:	What else?
7.	Adam:	Shoelace.
8.	Adam:	Pant.
9.	Adam:	Shoes.
10.	Adam:	Shoelace.

11.	Mother:	What else?
12.	Adam:	Shoelace.
13.	Mother:	Shoelace.
14.	Mother:	What else?
15.	Adam:	Pant.
16.	Adam:	Sock.
17.	Adam:	Dat socks.
18.	Adam:	Sock.
19.	Mother:	What else?
20.	Adam:	Face.
21.	Adam:	What else?
22.	Adam:	Cromer face.
23.	Mother:	**Cromer's face?**
24.	Adam:	Ursula's face.
25.	Adam:	Adam face.
26.	Mother:	What else?
27.	Adam:	Mommy face.
28.	Adam:	Mommy has a sock on.
29.	Mother:	No # I haven't on.
30.	Adam:	Cromer has a sock on.
31.	Adam:	Ursula has a boot on.
32.	Mother:	Ursula has **boots** on.
33.	Adam:	Have shoes on.
34.	Adam:	Eyes.
35.	Mother:	Eyes?
36.	Mother:	How many eyes?
37.	Adam:	Four.
38.	Mother:	Four eyes.
39.	Mother:	How many ears?
40.	Adam:	Four.
41.	Mother:	Four ears.
42.	Adam:	How many nose?
43.	Mother:	Yes # how many **noses?**
44.	Adam:	Four.
45.	Mother:	Four.
46.	Mother:	How many mouths?
47.	Adam:	Mouth # Cathy # pop go weasel.

As you can see, Adam's mother adds a missing verb (line 2), a missing plural suffix (lines 4, 32, 43), and a missing possessive marker (line 23).

How serious are parents about recasting?

Although recasts LOOK helpful, mothers don't provide them all that consistently. (Fathers and even older siblings provide recasts too, but perhaps not as frequently as mothers do.[11])

In one study of forty mothers of children aged two to five, it was found that only mothers of the two year olds actually recast children's "bad" utterances significantly more often than their "good" sentences. And, as the following table shows, even they provided recasts only about a quarter of the time (26.3 percent, to be exact).

Recast rates for mothers of two-year-old children[12]

	"bad" sentences	"good" sentences
% of times repeated in whole or in part	**26.3**	13.7
% of times not repeated	73.7	86.3

With numbers like these, it would be pretty hard for two-year-olds to RELY on their mother's recasts to learn language. In fact, it might even be misleading. Not only do mothers leave the vast majority of their children's bad sentences alone (73.7 percent in this sample), they sometimes partially repeat and change perfectly good utterances (13.7 percent).

You can see both of these things happening in the speech sample we just looked at. On the one hand, Adam's mother makes no attempt to recast a number of his incorrect utterances – *dat socks* in line 17 and *Adam face* in line 25, for example.

On the other hand, she recasts two utterances that were fine to begin with – Adam's *four* in lines 37 and 40 is perfectly okay as it stands. There is no need to add a noun like *eyes* or *ears* after the numeral in English (although some languages do require this).

To complicate matters still further, there are even times when mothers repeat their child's imperfect utterances, as if they approved of them. You can see an example of this in the following conversation, in which Adam's mother repeats his incomplete *read book* without adding the missing *the* or *a*. (Adam was twenty-eight months old at the time.)

Adam: Book.
Adam: Read book.
Mother: Alright, you **read book**.

This type of thing is surprisingly common. One study reports that mothers may repeat as many as one third of their children's incorrect utterances without making any changes.[13]

Do recasts help?

In light of this, it's perhaps not surprising that recasts are not a magical elixir. They don't always have a discernible effect, at least not a reliable one.

In line 23 of our speech sample, for instance, Adam's mother provides a recast that models the possessive marker -'*s*, which Adam then includes in his next utterance (line 24) but drops in the following one (line 25).

22.   Adam: Cromer face.
23.   Mother: Cromer**'s** face?
24.   Adam: Ursula**'s** face.
25.   Adam: Adam face.

The effectiveness of recasts is dubious in other cases as well. Take definite and indefinite articles (*the* and *a*), for example. Young children often drop these words, and parents sometimes respond with a recast that includes the missing element.

CHILD: Clown fall down.
PARENT: Yes, **the** clown fell down.

But does this make a difference?

One study focused on this question by examining the relationship between article use and recasts in the speech of three children.[14] The researchers found that the children's parents provided recasts for missing articles about 35 percent of the time. However, this seemed to have no immediate effect. The children didn't suddenly start using articles in response to their parent's recasts.

In addition, there was no link between the frequency of recasts and the rate at which children's use of articles increased over the longer term. No matter how many recasts children heard, it didn't seem to speed up their learning of articles.

On the other hand, we do know that recasts are sometimes effective. In one especially intriguing experiment,[15] four- and five-year-olds were taught "fake" verbs that referred to various funny actions (such as bopping someone with a beanbag attached to a string).

When the children first learned the verbs, they heard only the "-*ing* forms" ("This is called *pelling*"), so they had no idea what the past tense forms should be. In fact, the verbs were supposed to be irregular, so that the past tense of *pell* was *pold*, not *pelled*. (The real verb *tell* works this way.)

Two strategies were used for teaching the past tense – one that allowed children to make a mistake and then hear a recast and the other that simply presented the correct form to begin with.

Strategy 1: Children are allowed to make a mistake and then hear a recast

ADULT: What happened?
CHILD: He pelled him.
ADULT: Yes, he POLD him

Strategy 2: Children are presented with the correct form to begin with

ADULT: Look what happened! He POLD him on the leg.

The results of this experiment were very clear. No new verb was ever used with the right past tense form by a child when it was presented using Strategy 2. However, Strategy 1 achieved a success rate of almost 30 percent after a single recast!

This suggests that children are sensitive to recasts, especially those that offer a *direct and immediate contrast* between the child's way of saying something and the adult way. (Notice that Strategy 1 presents the child with "pold" right after she says "pelled.")

A longer-term study, involving ten sessions over a five-week period, yielded even more impressive results.[16] By the end of the fifth week, children had a success rate of almost 100 percent when exposed to recasts, compared to only about 40 percent when they did not receive this type of feedback.

A question of timing

Recasts may be more helpful at certain points in the learning process than at others. A detailed study of Eve showed that she was most sensitive to recasts at the point where she was already using the correct form about 50 percent of the time.[17] Prior to then, recasts didn't seem to make much difference. But from that point on, she was more likely to modify her speech in response to recasts.

It may be, then, that recasts are more useful for remembering to use the forms that have already been learned than for learning new forms. If this is right, it means that recasts don't help children *learn* language. They just help them get better at *using* what they've already managed to learn.

This seems reasonable. If recasts were the key to language learning, we'd expect some children to be more successful at language learning than others since some parents provide more recasts than others.[18]

But this just isn't so: children learn language successfully under a wide range of very different conditions. There even seem to be cultures in which children are not treated as conversational partners until they can produce sentences of their own – recasts for such children are probably a rare luxury at best, but they still learn their language without any noticeable difficulty or delay.[19]

So it looks like recasts are HELPFUL but that they are not NECESSARY. Children can learn language without them or any other sort of teaching.

3. So, what DO children need?

What then do children need from their parents? If children don't try to imitate their parents (at least for sentences), and if they don't rely on them for teaching or even recasts, what's the point of having adults around at all?

It has been suggested that one of the ways in which parents contribute to language acquisition is by speaking to children in a special way. Called *motherese*, this type of speech is characterized by slow, careful articulation and the use of basic vocabulary items, short sentences, and somewhat exaggerated intonation.

Some properties of motherese[20]

Pronunciation:

- Slower speech with longer pauses between utterances and after content words
- Higher overall pitch; greater pitch range
- Exaggerated intonation and stress
- Fewer words per minute

Vocabulary and meaning:

- More restricted vocabulary
- Three times as much paraphrasing
- More reference to the here and now

Sentences:

- Fewer broken or run-on sentences
- Shorter, less complex utterances (approx. 50 percent are single words or short statements)
- More well-formed and intelligible sentences
- More commands and questions (approx. 60 percent of total)
- More repetitions

Fathers and siblings adjust their speech too, by the way, but not as much as mothers do.[21]

It's easy to see how the sorts of adjustments associated with motherese could be helpful to children. Slow, careful articulation makes speech easier to perceive and to break down into smaller parts. Restricted vocabulary, short sentences, and a focus on the here and now should make speech easier to comprehend. And the use of repetitions gives children a second chance to understand what has been said.

Plus, it's known that children are attracted by motherese – four-month-olds will turn their heads more frequently toward speech with the intonation of motherese than to speech with more adult-like intonation.[22] (As far as I know, the magnetic power of fatherese has not yet been investigated.)

Does motherese help?

Perhaps. As just noted, many of the features of motherese seem designed to enhance the comprehensiblity of the mother's speech – which makes sense, since most mothers want to COMMUNICATE with their children. Being exposed to highly comprehensible speech in the early stages of language acquisition can't hurt.

However, that doesn't mean that motherese is NECESSARY for language acquisition to occur. In fact, we know that it CANNOT be necessary. That's because there are communities and cultures in which motherese is used little if at all.[23]

For example, in the course of her extensive research in the Afro-American working-class town of Trackton during the 1970s, Shirley Brice Heath noticed that adults there don't simplify their speech at all when addressing children. They don't use simple words or baby talk, and they don't speak any slower than usual.[24]

In fact, Heath reports, adults in Trackton don't even see babies or young children as suitable partners for regular conversation. Except for warnings, teasing, and orders, she says, "adults rarely address speech specifically to very young children."[25] Yet Trackton children learn language.

This flies in the face of standard (mis)conceptions about children and language, I know. Every society has its myths, and one of ours is that children need special help learning language. Steven Pinker has attempted to put this in perspective by noting a bit of folklore from another culture.[26] The !Kung Sang of Africa's Kalahari Desert, he reports, believe that children must be taught to sit, stand, and walk. Of course, the !Kung Sang are wrong about that – children sit, stand, and walk on their own when they're ready.

And we're wrong about language – children learn to speak without any special help too. Annie Mae, a Trackton resident, explains it this way when asked how she expected her grandson to learn to talk:[27]

He's got to learn to know about this world; there's no one who can tell him . . . White folks hear their kids say something, they say it back to them, they ask them again and again about things, like they're supposed to be born knowing. You think I can tell Teegie [her grandson] all that he's got to know to get along? He's just got to be keen, keep his eyes open . . . There's no use me telling him, "Learn this, learn that. What's this? What's that?"

What really matters

Does this mean that children can learn language no matter what their circumstances? Not quite. There's at least one external condition that must be met before language can be acquired. *Children need to hear sentences that they can understand without knowing a lot about the language they're trying to learn.*[28]

You can see why this is so if you think about the following simple question: could you learn a language just by listening to it on the radio?

The answer, of course, is no. If you had a really great memory, you might be able to memorize certain chunks of speech, especially if you heard them often enough. But you'd never know what anything meant. You wouldn't know whether the chunk you memorized was a word or a sentence, or whether subjects come before verbs or after them. You wouldn't know how to make nouns plural, or how to put verbs in the past tense.

The whole thing would be pointless and hopeless, and you'd probably give up pretty quickly. And so would a child. In fact, it's been reported that hearing children growing up in homes with non-speaking deaf parents cannot learn language from radio or even television.[29]

But now imagine a different scenario. Let's say that after listening to your mother and others around you for a few months, you've managed to learn a couple of dozen common words – mostly names for things that you often look at, touch, or play with. (Recall that most of a child's first words are in fact nouns of just this type.)

Assume one of those words is *doggie* and that on a particular day you are looking out the window with your mother when a dog runs by. Your mother says, "Look. The doggie is running." You miss the little word in front of *doggie* and the little word in front of *running*, neither of which is stressed and neither of which carries a concrete meaning. But you catch the familiar word *doggie*. And you catch the word *running* (or at least the *run* part), and you match it to what the dog is doing.

In that instant, you've made two important steps forward – you've learned a verb (*run*) and you've seen that it comes after its subject in English. And all this happened because you were able to figure out the meaning of your mother's sentence just by looking at what was happening around you. You didn't have to know the entire language already to understand what she said.

Now, of course, not all the several million sentences a child hears during the first three years of her life[30] are going to be as transparent as this one – a child might overhear her mother say "A cut in the tax on dividend earnings makes bad economic sense," for example. Sentences like that are simply going to zip by without doing any harm or any good.

But quite a large portion of speech to children is about what they can see or hear, what they want to know about, and what they have just experienced or are about to experience.[31] It's this type of speech that provides children with the raw material they need to learn a language. (Parents take note!)

This works in Trackton too, by the way. Even though adults there address speech to children relatively infrequently, they are often with children and they do speak in front of them to others.[32] So long as at least some of those sentences are about the here and now and therefore are comprehensible to children, the key condition for language acquisition is in place. (Do young Trackton children pay attention to those sorts of sentences? Evidently they do, since Heath reports that they frequently repeat them.)

But regardless of whether it's Seattle or Trackton, we still have to ask "Then what?" You could produce easy-to-understand sentences in front of a cat for all nine of its lives, and it still wouldn't learn English. Obviously, there's more to language learning than just hearing certain types of sentences in certain types of contexts. That something cannot be observed so directly, though, because it's inside the child's head.

4. It's all in the head

Everyone pretty well agrees that human beings are especially suited to learn language. Part of the reason for this is that they have the right type of lips, tongues, throats, and noses. Language sounds the way it does because of our speech organs and because of the way we use them.

A creature that had a long thin tongue (like a dog), or no lips (like a cat), or less muscular vocal cords (like a chimpanzee), or less well-developed connections between the brain and the muscles of the mouth and throat (like all animals except us) just wouldn't be able to produce the sounds that are found in human languages.

Language would also be inaccessible to a species that didn't have the type of ears and auditory centers in the brain that we have. There wouldn't be a way to process speech sounds or recognize the patterns that they contain.

Most important of all, only a creature with a human brain is able to break those patterns into smaller parts – words, roots, prefixes, and suffixes, determine what each one means, and then figure out how to assemble them in novel ways to say new things.

When I say a human brain, I mean a brain constructed in accordance with the instructions contained in our DNA. Which in turn means that the capacity for language is part of our genetic inheritance. There's ample evidence that this must be so, and some of the best evidence comes from language disorders. The key idea is simply that if the capacity for language is inherited, then there should be such a thing as inherited language disorders too.

This makes a good deal of sense. After all, if children can be near-sighted, why couldn't they be born with a flawed linguistic system – especially if language, like vision, is an inherited capacity? The question is where to look for such disorders and how to be sure that they are caused by genetic factors rather than by something in the child's environment, such as parents who are abusive or neglectful in some way.

When things go wrong

One of the most promising sources of evidence for inherited language disorders comes from the study of identical twins. The key finding to date is very suggestive: identical twins are significantly more similar to each other in their linguistic abilities and disabilities than are fraternal or non-identical twins.[33]

There is no apparent environmental explanation for this finding, since twins of both types grow up in the same household and presumably receive approximately the same exposure to language in the early years of life. But there is a genetic explanation: identical twins have the same genes and therefore should be alike with respect to capacities that are shaped by the operation of those genes.

Another place to look for signs of an inherited language capacity is in studies of adopted children. All other things being equal, we'd expect the linguistic abilities of adopted children to be closer to those of their biological relatives than to those of their adopted relatives, with whom they live.

Here again the evidence is suggestive. Adopted children with biological relatives who have a language disorder are almost three times as likely to suffer from language disorders than adopted children whose relatives are not linguistically impaired. Like the twin studies, these results offer evidence for an inherited capacity for language that can be flawed in various ways.[34]

There are even cases of language disorders that have actually been linked to a specific gene. One case of this type that has garnered a considerable amount of attention in recent years involves three generations of a London-based family known as KE.

Of the twenty-nine family members who have been tested so far, fourteen suffer from an inherited language disorder that impairs a variety of linguistic skills, most notably the ability to correctly use regular suffixes such as plural *-s* and past tense *-ed*.

Family members with this disorder repeat the word *bees* as *bee* – although they don't have any trouble saying the word *nose*, in which the final "z" sound is not a suffix. They also produce sentences with strange plural and tense mismatches, like "It's a flying finches, they are" and "She remembered when she hurts herself the other day." And, perhaps most interesting of all, they fail the "*wug* test" – they have great trouble producing the plural and past tense forms of novel words.[35]

In 2001, two Oxford geneticists identified the gene underlying this disorder – FOXP2, whose function is to switch on various other genes.[36] It's tempting to think that a particular gene might be responsible for a particular part of language (like the ability to add inflectional endings),[37] but genes usually don't work that way. Their effect is typically much more indirect.

It's likely that FOXP2 works indirectly too – it does something that results in something that leads to a language disorder. And sure enough, there is evidence that members of the KE family with the defective gene have problems that extend well beyond inflectional endings and even beyond language.

Not only is their speech almost unintelligible due to articulatory problems, they are unable to imitate facial movements such as opening the mouth and sticking out the tongue. In addition, their IQs are on average 18 or 19 points lower than those of unaffected family members.[38]

5. The search for the acquisition device

Even after geneticists identify the particular genes that shape the brain's ability to learn and use language, a question will remain – the question of how language is acquired.

That's because answering this question involves more than identifying genes. It involves figuring out exactly what the brain of an infant DOES when it is exposed to speech and how that results in a fully fluent child three years later.

Unfortunately, the brain is not easy to study directly. In fact, a lot of what we know about its role in language comes from studying what happens when it is damaged as the result of a stroke or a wound. And almost all of the rest comes from experiments done with healthy adults – using electrodes, brain scans, and other techniques that don't require surgery. When it comes to figuring out what it is about children's brains that makes them so good at learning language, we have to adopt a different strategy.

That strategy is to think of the brain as if it were a "black box." That's a term that scientists sometimes use to describe a device whose contents cannot be directly observed. The part of the black box that is concerned with language learning is sometimes called the *acquisition device*.

We have a pretty good idea of what gets fed into it – as we saw a short while ago, the most essential ingredient seems to be just hearing people talk about understandable things. Let's just call this "experience."

We also have a pretty good idea of what the black box churns out – the knowledge needed to use a language. Linguists often call this knowledge a *grammar*. You probably think of a grammar as something that's written in a book, but linguists use it to mean "knowledge of a language."

If this is right, then the language learning process comes down to something like this.

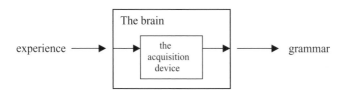

The job of language acquisition researchers is to figure out precisely what's in the little black box labeled "acquisition device" that turns experience into knowledge.

To some extent, of course, the acquisition device is an abstraction. It's not literally a box in the brain. In fact, it's likely that its parts are spread out in different regions of the brain, just as books about language can be found in different parts of a library.

For now, the key to thinking about the acquisition device is to focus on what those parts are and how they work. And here there are two very different views.

View # 1: The acquisition device is just for language

According to one view, the acquisition device has a very specific language-oriented design that makes it good for just one thing – language acquisition.

In fact, according to some versions of this view, like those put forward by Noam Chomsky, the acquisition device includes a pre-made (i.e. inborn) grammar.[39] This is generally called *Universal Grammar*, because it consists of the sorts of grammatical categories and principles that are common to all languages.

Being born with such a system would give children a huge head start when it comes to language learning. Take categories, for instance.

The difference between nouns and verbs is one of the most fundamental and important contrasts in all of language. But discovering this and figuring out which words belong in which category is more challenging than you might think.

The problem comes down to knowing what to look for. Take the following sentence, for example.

That dog is misbehaving.

Dog is a noun and *misbehave* is a verb, but how is a child supposed to figure that out?

There are many differences between the two words. *Dog* begins with the "d" sound, it refers to an animal, it consists of just one syllable, it occurs next to the "locator" word *that*, it appears in the second position in the sentence, and so on. If you didn't know anything about language, how would you know which of these properties are important for categorizing words and which are not?

What would prevent you from setting up a system of word classes in which all the words beginning with the "d" sound go together – *dog, do, dull, dangle*, and so on? Or what would prevent you from putting the words *dog, already, at*, and *see* in the same class simply because they can all occur in the second position in a sentence?

The DOG bit me.
I ALREADY ate.
Look AT the giraffe.
I SEE the elephant.

In other words, why would a child even think of grouping words into noun and verb classes? And even if she did, how would she know which words are nouns and which ones are verbs?

The answer that linguists favoring Universal Grammar have come up with is that the acquisition device tells children what to do and what to look for. In particular, it tells them that all languages are going to have particular categories (nouns and verbs, for example) and it gives them some clues that help them figure out which words belong to which category.[40]

Clues to categories

What might these clues look like? One possibility is that they involve information about the type of meaning most often associated with particular word classes. For example, the acquisition device might "tell" children that words referring to concrete things must be nouns. So language learners would know right away that words like *dog*, *boy*, *house*, and *tree* belong to that word class.

This might just be enough to get started. Once children knew what some nouns looked like, they could start noticing other things on their own – like the fact that items in the noun class can occur with locator words like *this* and *that*, that they can take the plural ending, that they can be used as subjects and direct objects, that they are usually stressed, and so on.

Nouns with locator words:	**That dog** looks tired.
	This house is ours.
Nouns with the plural ending:	**Cats** make me sneeze.
	I like **cookies**.
Nouns used as subject or direct object:	**Dogs** chase **cats**.
	A **man** painted our **house**.

Information of this sort can then be used to deal with words like *idea* and *attitude*, which cannot be classified on the basis of their meaning. (They are nouns, but they don't refer to concrete things.) Sooner or later a child will hear these words used with *this* or *that*, or with a plural, or in a subject position. If she's learned that these are the signs of nounhood, it'll be easy to recognize nouns that don't refer to concrete things.

If all of this is on the right track, then the procedure for iden-tifying words belonging to the noun class would go something like this. (Similar procedures exist for verbs, adjectives, and other categories.)

What the acquisition device tells the child	What the child then notices	What the child can then do
If a word refers to a concrete object, it's a noun.	Noun words can also occur with *this* and *that*; they can be pluralized; they can be used as subjects and direct objects.	Identify less typical nouns (*idea*, *attitude*, etc.) based on how they are used in sentences.

This whole process is sometimes called *bootstrapping* (a process considered in a different context in chapter 3). The basic idea is that the acquisition device gives the child a little bit of information to get started (e.g., a language must distinguish between nouns and verbs; if a word refers to a concrete object, it's a noun) and then leaves her to pull herself up the rest of the way by these bootstraps.

Blueprints for sentences

By themselves, of course, words are just building blocks. To be of any real use, they have to be put together in the right way. And that calls for a blueprint. Take a simple sentence like *Jean helped Roger*, for instance.

Obviously, the three words – and their meanings – must combine with each other. But how does this happen? Does the verb combine directly with the two nouns?

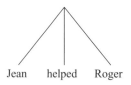

Or does it combine first with its subject, forming a larger building block that then combines with the direct object?

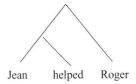

Jean   helped   Roger

Or does it perhaps combine first with its direct object, creating a building block that then combines with the subject?

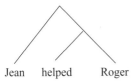

Jean   helped   Roger

How could a child possibly figure out which of these design options is right? For that matter, how could an adult?

Once again, the acquisition device must come to the rescue by providing the following vital bits of information.

- Words are grouped into pairs.
- Subjects (doers) are higher than direct objects (undergoers).

With this information in hand, it's easy for children to build sentences with the right design. Good engineering starts with good blueprints.

View # 2: The acquisition device is not just for language

The other idea about the acquisition device is the exact opposite. It claims that the acquisition device is not designed just for language. Rather, it is "a new machine made up of old parts," to use a metaphor suggested by Elizabeth Bates and Brian MacWhinney.[41] That is, it can handle language, but its various parts are not specialized for just that task.

Take the Mutual Exclusivity Assumption, for example. As we saw in chapter 3, mutual exclusivity ensures that things should have just one label. That's why a child who is shown an object whose name she knows (a banana, say) and a new object (a whisk, for example) and is then asked "Show me the fendle" will point to the new object.[42]

But is Mutual Exclusivity just for words and their meanings? Perhaps not. Paul Bloom suggests that it's really just an example of a very general sort of reasoning that goes something like this:[43]

1. I know that a banana is called *banana*.
2. If the speaker meant to refer to the banana, she would have asked me to show her the banana.
3. But she didn't; she used the strange word *fendle*.
4. So she must intend to refer to something other than the banana.
5. A plausible candidate is the whisk.
6. *Fendle* must refer to the whisk.

This type of reasoning is not just used for words and meanings; it's used for information in general.

Gil Disendruck and Lori Markson conducted an experiment in which three-year-olds were shown two objects and given some novel information about one of them – like "My sister gave this to me." When then asked "Can you show me the one that dogs like to play with?" they tended to choose the second object. The reasoning here seems parallel.[44]

1. I know that the first object came from the speaker's sister.
2. If the speaker meant to refer to that object, she would have asked me to show her the one that her sister gave her.
3. But she didn't; she asked for the object that dogs like to play with.
4. So she must intend to refer to something other than the first object.
5. A plausible candidate is the second object.
6. The second object must be the one that dogs likes to play with.

Bloom claims that word learning strategies in general work this way – none of them is used just for learning the meaning of words.[45]

Statistical learning

Another example of a more general tool that is part of the acquisition device involves "statistical learning" – keeping track of the relative probability of two or more things happening together.

As we saw in chapter 2, a series of dazzling experiments by Peter Jusczyk and his colleagues suggest that infants who are not yet able to speak have nonetheless figured out that words have particular phonetic properties.

One of these is stress – most two-syllable nouns in English have the "strong–weak" stress pattern heard in BAby and DOCtor. Another involves the type of consonant combinations that occur at word boundaries – the sequence "ng-t," for instance, is common between words (as in *wrong time*), but not inside words.

Similar abilities have been observed for grammar. As noted in chapter 4, for example, eighteen-month-olds prefer to listen to passages containing *is* + *Verb-ing* patterns rather than *can* + *Verb-ing* patterns. Their own speech still consists largely of one-word utterances, but somehow they have already observed a tendency for *is* and *Verb-ing* to occur together in adult speech.

These are all remarkable accomplishments and no doubt important for learning a language, since it matters a great deal where word boundaries are and which items occur together. But there is no reason to think that the ability to note statistical correlations of this sort is restricted to language learning. Many things are learned that way – the relationship between dogs and barking, clouds and rain, doctor visits and needles, and so on.

So which view is correct?

The debate between those who think that there is an acquisition device just for language and those who believe in a more general sort of learning mechanism has been going on for at least thirty years. During much of this time, the two camps have talked past each other, with each focusing on different phenomena.

The above examples illustrate this nicely – the argument in favor of a just-for-language acquisition device involves categories and structures, while the examples in favor of a more general acquisition device involve words and their meanings.

So why don't the two camps just go "head to head" on the same phenomenon – say syntactic categories and structures? The answer is that they can't agree on what syntactic categories and structures are like in the first place. And without that agreement, it's not possible to have a debate about how they are acquired.

The dispute over the nature of the acquisition device is really part of a much deeper disagreement over the nature of language itself.

On the one hand, there are linguists who see language as a highly complex formal system that is best described by abstract rules that have no counterparts in other areas of cognition. (The requirement that sentences have a binary branching syntactic structure is one example of such a "rule.") Not surprisingly, there is a strong tendency for these researchers to favor the view that the acquisition device is designed specifically for language.

On the other hand, there are many linguists who think that language has to be understood in terms of its communicative function. According to these researchers, strategies that facilitate communication – not abstract formal rules – determine how language works. Because communication involves many different types of considerations (new versus old information, point of view, the status of speaker and addressee, the situation), this perspective tends to be associated with a bias toward a multipurpose acquisition device.

The disagreement over the nature of language has been going on for even longer than the dispute over the nature of the acquisition device. Unfortunately, it is not likely to be settled any time soon. However, there are still a lot of things we can learn in the meantime about how language acquisition works. One of them – and the final topic for this book – involves the learning process itself.

6. Learning to learn

Regardless of how much is built into the acquisition device, there's still a lot about language that has to be learned. Even if the acquisition device tells children that words referring to concrete objects are nouns in whatever language they're learning, they're on their own when it comes to figuring out what the plural form of a noun looks like.

In English, the plural is signaled by the suffix *-s*, but not all languages work that way. In Korean, the plural is marked by the optional suffix *-tul* (*namja* can mean either "man" or "men"; *namja-tul* is unambiguously "men"). In Tagalog, on the other hand, the plural is formed by adding the prefix *mga* (*bata* is "child," *mga bata* is "children"). In Indonesian, it's indicated by repeating the noun (*orang* is "man" and *orang orang* is "men").

Some things that children learning English must figure out for themselves

- The plural is usually formed by adding *-s* (*book*/*books*), but there are some exceptions (*men*, *children*, *fish*, and so forth).
- The past tense is usually formed by adding *-ed* (*walk*/*walked*), but there are a lot of exceptions (*ran*, *ate*, *slept*, *lost*, *did*, *fell*, *saw*, and so on).
- A verb combines with its subject and direct object in the order subject–verb–direct object (*The cat drank the milk.*).
- A noun combines with an adjective and an article in the order article–adjective–noun (*a big truck*).
- Questions are formed by moving a light verb to the front of the sentence (*Can you stay?*).

Evidently, then, the acquisition device has to be powerful enough and flexible enough to allow children to master a huge number of facts about whatever language they happen to be learning. There's a well-known learning procedure that can help. It's often simply called *generalization*, because it involves drawing a general conclusion from specific cases.

Conservative estimates

Generalization is a very useful and very commonplace learning strategy. You use it when you see three or four sheep and then conclude that all sheep are woolly and eat grass. And you use it when you conclude that you are allergic to chocolate if you break out in hives for the third time in a row right after eating it.

The ability to generalize gives children a powerful learning tool. It allows them to notice words like *dogs*, *books*, and *cars*, and then conclude that *-s* can be added to a noun to indicate "more than one." It allows them to notice words like *walked*, *jumped*, and *danced* and then conclude that *-ed* can be added to a verb to form the past tense. And it allows them to hear sentences like *Mommy seems tired* and *Kitty is hungry* and then conclude that you can make a sentence by putting together a noun, a verb, and an adjective in that order.

But generalization is so powerful that it has the potential to run amok. For example, a child shouldn't conclude that just because the words *Mommy*, *seems*, and *tired* can go together, any three words can go together, or that they can go together in any order. *Mommy seems jumped* isn't an English sentence, and neither is *Tired seems Mommy*.

Somehow, children avoid mistakes of this sort. Evidently, there is a way to control generalization so that it doesn't go too far too fast. But how precisely does this work?

A number of linguists have suggested that the generalization process is subject to a "Be Conservative" Law that forces children to be cautious in deciding what their language allows.[46]

The "Be Conservative" Law
Make "small" generalizations; don't overgeneralize.

Take word order, for example. Some languages, like English, have a relatively fixed word order. The subject precedes the verb and the verb precedes the direct object.

John read the book.

In contrast, word order in Spanish is very flexible. The subject can come at the beginning of the sentence (like in English), right after the verb, or at the end of the sentence.

subject at the beginning	subject after the verb	subject at the end
Juan leyó el libro	Leyó **Juan** el libro	Leyó el libro **Juan**
John read the book	Read John the book	Read the book John

But how does a child figure out that English has only one word order, the one found in *John read the book*? By making the conservative estimate, children avoid producing word orders that they don't actually hear.

Being conservative in these types of learning situations makes a lot of sense. Errors can take a lot of time and effort to correct, so the safe course of action is to be cautious and to assume that if you don't hear a particular pattern, then it can't be said.

In fact, if you go back to chapter 4, you'll find some evidence there that confirms just how conservative children are when it comes to word order. Remember that we looked into the question of whether children start out by learning "little" word order rules (like "Put the subject in front of *push*") or a "big" one (like "Put the subject in front of any verb").

The evidence showed that children are very cautious at age two and rely heavily on little rules. It is only around age four, after several years of experience with language, that they dare formulate the big generalization that all subjects come before verbs in English.

Getting out of trouble

Although children are highly conservative when it comes to things like word order patterns, they don't seem to be quite so cautious with other things, like the use of particular words or endings. Here, the temptation to follow a general pattern can sometimes prove too strong. Over-regularized plural forms like *mans*, *sheeps*, and *childs* and past tense forms like *eated*, *runned*, *sleeped*, *falled*, and *goed* are good examples of this, but they are not the only type of overgeneralization that shows up.

For instance, when my daughter was three years old, I used to take her to the playground every Saturday and Sunday and say to her something like "Let's play here for a while." One Saturday when we were having a lot of fun, she asked me if perhaps we could play "for two whiles."

It's pretty obvious what she was thinking – *while* should be like other nouns denoting periods of time (e.g., *minute*, *hour*, *day*). They can be counted (*a minute*, *two minutes*), so *while* can too. That was a perfectly reasonable assumption; it just wasn't right.

I didn't correct my daughter, because I wanted to see how all of this was going to turn out. So, I made a note of the error and started listening for other examples. I heard a couple more, but after a few weeks my daughter just stopped talking about "two whiles," and went back to saying just "a while."

Somehow, she must have realized that no one else was ever counting whiles.[47] Evidently, children are able to notice that there are certain things that other people don't say.

Doing goodly

Let's think about another example. When my daughter was four years old, she started using the word *goodly* where adults would say *well*.

We have to do this goodly.
Didn't I draw this goodly?

She did this quite systematically, and it is pretty easy to see what caused this error. She noticed the following quite general pattern involving adjectives (words that express properties of things) and adverbs (words that describe properties of actions).

Adjectives	Adverbs
quiet (a quiet man)	quiet**ly** (eat quietly)
slow (a slow car)	slow**ly** (go slowly)
happy (a happy girl)	happi**ly** (play happily)
quick (a quick dog)	quick**ly** (run quickly)

As you can see, there's a strong tendency in English for adverbs to be formed from adjectives by adding the -*ly* ending. My daughter obviously noticed this (language learners are SUPPOSED to notice general tendencies). She then used the generalization procedure to conclude that if there is an adjective *good*, there should be an adverb *goodly*. That was wrong, but it was not an unreasonable thing to do. The question is how to get back on track.

Once again, I did nothing to correct her mistake. And sure enough, after a few months she stopped saying *goodly* and started saying *well*. Her brakes (the "Be Conservative" Law) had failed, but fortunately her acquisition device had a back-up. Somehow, she was able to notice that no one else ever said *goodly*.

One thing that might have helped her is a learning strategy called the "Principle of Contrast."[48]

The Principle of Contrast
Every two forms contrast in meaning.

What this principle basically says is that no two words should have exactly the same meaning.

Sure, there are words that mean ALMOST the same thing – *slim*, *thin*, and *skinny*, for example – but there's always at least a subtle difference. (That's why we talk about thin hair and a slim waistline, and not the reverse.) Having these sorts of contrasts makes sense, since it would be uneconomical for a language to have words with exactly the same meaning and use.

In the case of *goodly*, the Principle of Contrast probably kicked in when my daughter heard me say things like "You did that really well" or "Did things go well today?" In these sentences, the word *well* had exactly the meaning that she would have expressed using *goodly*. The Principle of Contrast would have told her "you can't have two words with exactly the same meaning; one of them has to go."

Which one is kept and which one gets tossed out? The acquisition device seems in general to realize that adult speakers of the language know best. When there is a conflict between a form that others use and a form that the child has made up on her own, the former one wins out. Gradually, *goodly* gets replaced by *well*, *eated* gets pushed out by *ate*, and the language of the adult becomes the language of the child.

Remember, though, that it takes a lot of exposures to the adult form before the transformation is complete – several hundred according to one estimate (see chapter 2, section 3). What if this doesn't happen, perhaps because the word is rarely used? Then the child's over-regularized form may survive, and the language begins to change. That's why we say *thrived* rather than *throve* (the original past tense of *thrive*) in contemporary English.[49]

Recasts again

The Principle of Contrast may be most effective and most useful when there are recasts – those partial repetitions of children's utterances that we discussed a little earlier in this chapter. That's because recasts give the child an opportunity to hear competing items in close proximity to each other: she says "The doggie EATED it all" and right away hears her mother respond with the recast "Oh, he ATE it all, did he?" It must be fairly easy to notice that *eated* is infringing on the territory of *ate* here, since both are being used to express the same meaning.

This violates the Principle of Contrast, and it's probably at this point that the child starts to have doubts about *eated*. Under continued bombardment from *ate*, the immature form begins to wither and eventually disappears completely.

7. A final word

So, where does all of this leave us? At the very least, with a collection of abilities that make it possible to learn language.

To begin, there's a very early ability to distinguish speech sounds from other types of sounds and from each other. And there's the ability, which starts to emerge around the age of twelve months, to produce those same speech sounds in an intelligible manner, stringing them together to form words and sentences.

For words, there is first of all the ability to pick the building blocks of language out of the speech stream. As we've seen, the Matching Strategy and the Spotlight Strategy seem to be implicated here in some way. But it's important not to forget that these are just names for more fundamental abilities. There'd be no Spotlight Strategy if children didn't have a remarkable ability to notice recurring stress patterns (like the strong–weak pattern of English) and to notice which combinations of consonants are most likely to occur at word boundaries.

For meaning, there's the amazing ability to "fast map" – to learn the meaning of a word on the basis of a single exposure to its use. This in turn implicates various other abilities. There would be no fast mapping if children didn't see the world the way adults do, if they couldn't figure out what the speaker is paying attention to as he speaks, and if they couldn't use linguistic clues to infer (for instance) that a zav must be a thing but that Zav has to be a person.

For sentences, there's the ability to note patterns of particular types (subject–verb–object constructions, passives, negatives, relative clauses), to see how they are built, and to figure out what they are used for.

And tying it all together is the ability to learn – to form generalizations that have a good chance of being right the first time and to make corrections when there's a mistake.

Many things in life yield up their mysteries and lose their fascination after a little bit of examination and analysis. Language is not like that. Although it has been probed and analyzed and studied for over two thousand years, we still understand relatively little about how it works. The mystery is compounded by the fact that every year, tens of millions of children around the world quickly and effortlessly go about the job of language learning, creating the puzzle that we've been considering in this book: how do they do it?

For now at least, there's no complete answer to this question. But this is perhaps one of those questions that is as enjoyable to ponder as it is to answer. And, unlike many of the puzzles that scientists like to investigate, this one hits very close to home.

Appendix 1   Keeping a diary and making tape recordings

The simplest and most basic type of naturalistic study in language acquisition research involves keeping a diary. All that is needed for this is a notebook, a pencil, and a little curiosity. The best time to start is probably when the child is ten months old or so – just when he's starting to produce his first words.

A basic diary includes a written record of the child's first words, the situation in which each was uttered, the date, and perhaps some information about its pronunciation and meaning.

The type and amount of information that you choose to include depends in part on what interests you the most. For example, if you're interested in how pronunciation develops (see chapter 6), you'll note information about what the child's words sound like. Here are some examples of this from the diary of my daughter's speech.

Date (19XX)	Child's word	Adult word
Sept. 24	wa	water
Oct. 16	poppy	pumpkin
Oct. 17	up	up
Nov. 11	buh	bug
	pah	porridge
Nov. 14	doa	door
Nov. 20	peaze	please
Dec. 10	bayuh	bear
Dec. 18	toe	toad

Notice that the words are spelled to reflect their pronunciation and that the adult form of the word is written after it to help me remember later what my daughter was trying to say.

On the other hand, if you're more interested in how word meaning develops (chapter 3), then you'll focus on information about how children use their words to refer to objects and actions. For example, when a child uses the word *dog*, you should note whether it refers to the family pet or to a dog that she saw on the street. And you should keep track of later uses of this word to see whether it is ever used for animals other than dogs (that is, whether there are overextensions). Here are two sample entries from a diary containing this type of information.

Date (19XX)	Child's word	Adult word	Comment
June 9	krakuh	cracker	said several times to refer to Japanese crackers; used a few days later to refer to Graham crackers.
June 24	G	MG	said on several occasions while pointing at the MG symbol on her father's shirt. Used on July 24 to refer to an actual MG roadster.

For the first few months after a child begins to talk, it may be possible to make note of each and every one of his utterances – at least his NEW utterances. But you probably won't be able to keep up once he starts to produce multi-word sentences.

As noted in chapter 1, from that point on, a diary is used mostly to make note of special developments (like the first question with the light verb at the beginning of the sentence) or unusual occurrences (perhaps an instance of pre-subject negation). As you read through the book, you should get lots of ideas about interesting things to watch for and keep track of.

Naturalistic studies of children who are in the two-word stage or later stages of language development typically rely on audio- or videotaping. Ideally, half-hour or full-hour recordings are made once every two weeks, although less frequent intervals (say once a month) can also provide very useful information. If you manage to make regular recordings over a two-year period beginning at around eighteen months, you'll end up with a great highlight reel of a child's linguistic growth.

As noted in chapter 1, there are advantages to video-taping children's speech, but if that's not practical for you, don't worry about it. Many of the great studies in the field of language acquisition research have made use of good old-fashioned audio recording. So, just go ahead and use a tape recorder if that's what you have.

The best time to do your taping is when the child is most likely to do a lot of talking – perhaps when you and he are playing with toys or looking at a picture book together. (See the boxed insert for some additional hints.)

Doing the taping itself is very easy. The hard part is writing out what's on the tape. (Linguists call this "transcribing" and they refer to the end result as a "transcript.") Unfortunately, this can be very time consuming and even professional researchers find that it often takes them five or more hours to transcribe a single hour of tape! You may not have the time to do that right away, especially if you have a young child or two at home. But at least if you do the tape recording now, you'll be able to go back to it later and analyze it at your leisure.

One thing that you should try to do right away, though, is take notes on the taping session. Write down the time and place, the names of the people who were present, the toys or books that the child was playing with, and what types of things you did and talked about. You'd be surprised how difficult it can be to figure out what's being said when you listen to a tape that was made weeks or even months earlier. Without the help of your notes, you won't be able to make sense of large parts of the conversation. (This is especially true if you have to rely on audiotapes rather than videotapes.)

Some tips on how to tape a child's speech[1]

- Make sure the microphone is in the right position to pick up the voice of the child and the voice of whoever he is talking with. If it's safe to do so, it's probably best to use a microphone that can be put in different places rather than the type that is built into the tape recorder itself.
- Children are most likely to talk freely and naturally when they are in a familiar place (like home) with people who they know well (other family members rather than, say, visitors).

- Don't restrict your recording to just one setting or just one conversational partner. Children say different types of things at mealtime and at playtime, when talking to siblings, when talking to their father, and when talking to their mother.
- Watch out for background noise. A radio or TV, water running in the bathtub, the noise of a dishwasher or a washing machine, and the sound of several children playing at a birthday party can all make your recording unintelligible.
- Don't forget to take notes about the setting and the activities of the participants as the conversation is taking place. Mark the time and date on your notes and on your cassette tape.
- Begin your transcription of the tape as soon as practical after the recording session is over.
- It's often possible to figure out unclear meanings by listening to the two or three lines that come right before or right after.

Tape transcripts can contain different levels of detail, depending on your interests and your time. Some involve detailed information about the child's pronunciation and about the structure of his words and sentences. Others provide little more than a written record of what was said.

Here's an example of a basic, no-frills transcript, made by a group of Harvard researchers and based on a tape recording of a boy named Adam when he was thirty months old. (%com indicates a comment added by the researcher to clarify the situation.)

Adam:	listen.
Mother:	listen to what?
%com:	dropping small blocks on the floor.
Adam:	dirty dishes.
Adam:	drop it cowboy boot.
Adam:	I drop it cowboy boot.
Adam:	I drop it cowboy boot.
Mother:	go pick them up.
Adam:	pick em up.
Adam:	you, Mommy.
Adam:	you.
Adam:	cowboy drop it boot.
Mother:	ok, pick those up.
Mother:	We'll put them up now.

Adam:	no, no.
Adam:	here, Mommy.
Adam:	ice cream cone.
Adam:	ice cream cone.
Mother:	Don't put them on the floor, Adam.
Adam:	doggie.
Mother:	Oh, that's for the doggie?
Adam:	just like cowboy.
Adam:	yeah.
Adam:	(a)nother one up.
Mother:	No, now pick the doggie up.
Mother:	He's finished.

You probably won't be able to transcribe each and every thing that is said in a particular taping session. Background noise, the quality of the recording, and unclear pronunciations can cause problems for even the most experienced transcriber. For example, in the following excerpt from the same tape, the Harvard researcher was unable to interpret something that Adam said (it's marked "xxx" in the second line below) and was uncertain about several other things (which are indicated by [?] symbols). (Ursula is Ursula Bellugi, one of several student researchers in the Harvard group who went on to become a well-known linguist.)

Ursula:	do you have some?
Adam:	no xxx have some.
Adam:	I don't [?] have some.
Adam:	d(o) you [?] have some.
Adam:	some dipping [?] vat [?] dipping [?] vat [?] cowboy dipping [?] vat [?].
Ursula:	sleeping bag?
Mother:	no, dipping vat!

How to calculate MLU

As we saw in chapter 4, keeping track of the mean length of a child's utterance (or MLU) provides a rough estimate of grammatical development. The first step in this calculation involves counting the meaning-bearing elements (or morphemes) in the child's sentences. Here are some general rules for doing this.[2]

- Do not try to analyze sentences that contain incomprehensible parts.
- If there is stuttering, count the repeated word only once.
- Do not count fillers such as *um* or *oh*, but do count *no*, *yeah*, and *hi*.
- Count compound words (*birthday*, *pocketbook*), names (*Mary Jane*), and reduplications (*night-night*) as one element.
- Count diminutives (*doggie*, *mommy*) as one element.
- Count contracted elements such as *gonna*, *hafta*, and *wanna* as one element.
- Count irregular past tense forms (*got*, *did*, *went*, etc.) as one element.

If we follow these guidelines, we will analyze the following four sentences from one of Adam's transcripts as follows. I place a dot under each meaningful element.

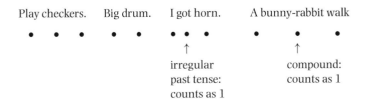

Here, then, we have a total of eleven meaningful elements in four utterances – which gives us an MLU of 2.75 (11 ÷ 4) for this tiny body of data.

Of course, real calculations of MLU are done with a much larger set of sentences – usually a minimum of 100. If you are lucky enough to have transcripts of the child you are studying, you may want to try MLU calculations for each transcription. Over a period of time, you'll notice a sharp increase in MLU – a sure sign of progress in his language development.

Appendix 2   The sounds of English

All speech sounds are made by varying the position of the tongue and the lips, and by controlling the actions of the larynx (or voice box). The figure below provides a side view of the human vocal tract, with various key parts labeled.

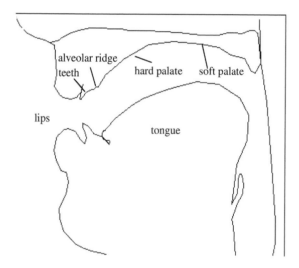

The charts that follow summarize the key properties of the consonant and vowel sounds used in most varieties of North American English, including the place in the vocal tract where each is produced. The pronunciation of the particular example words used here may be different in other varieties of English, especially for the vowels.

Consonant sounds

(An asterisk indicates that the sound is voiced – i.e., produced with vocal-cord vibrations.)

Symbol	Examples	Location in the mouth
[p]	pie, hop	lips
[b]*	bat, mob	lips
[m]*	my, him	lips
[f]	fee, off	lower lip, upper teeth
[v]*	vice, of	lower lip, upper teeth
[θ]	thing, bath	tip of the tongue between the teeth, or against the back of the upper front teeth
[ð]*	this, bathe	tip of the tongue between the teeth, or against the back of the upper front teeth
[t]	tie, eat	tip of the tongue against the alveolar ridge
[d]*	die, bid	tip of the tongue against the alveolar ridge
[n]*	no, on	tip of the tongue against the alveolar ridge
[s]	sun, pass	front part of the tongue touching lightly against the alveolar ridge
[z]*	zip, haze	front part of the tongue touching lightly against the alveolar ridge
[r]*	rip, car	tip of the tongue bent slightly back and held near (but not quite touching) the alveolar ridge
[l]*	lip, call	tip of the tongue against the alveolar ridge
[ʃ] or [š]	shy, ash	front part of the tongue touching lightly against the back of the alveolar ridge/front of the hard palate
[ʒ] or [ž]*	measure	front part of the tongue touching lightly against the back of the alveolar ridge/front of the hard palate
[č] or [tʃ]	chip, rich	front part of the tongue against the back of the alveolar ridge/front of the hard palate
[ĵ] or [ʤ]*	Joe, age	front part of the tongue against the back of the alveolar ridge/front of the hard palate

[k]	kite, back	back of the tongue against the soft palate
[g]*	go, big	back of the tongue against the soft palate
[ŋ]*	sing	back of the tongue against the soft palate
[h]	hot	in the voice box (air from the lungs rushes between the vocal cords creating light friction)
[w]*	wet	the back of the tongue is high in the mouth; the lips are rounded
[y] or [j]*	yes	the body of the tongue is high in the mouth, near the front part of the hard palate

Vowel sounds

Symbol	Examples	Location of the tongue
[i]	he, cream, teen	high, front
[I]	hit, been	high, front
[e]	they, clay, stain, sane	mid, front
[ɛ]	led, head, says, said	mid, front
[æ]	pat, laugh	low, front
[u]	to, two, too, Sue	high, back
[ʊ]	put, would, stood	high, back
[o]	so, coat, though	mid, back
[ɔ]†	caught, bought	mid, back
[ɑ]	cot, caught, father	low, back
[ʌ]	shut, rough, was, blood	mid, central
[ə]	sof<u>a</u>, witch<u>e</u>s, hunt<u>e</u>d	mid, central (unstressed syllables only)

†Not found in all varieties of North American English

Notes

1. Small talk

1. These examples are from http://www.rinkworks.com/said/kidquotes. shtml.
2. From the speech of Sarah, at age three and a half.
3. MacWhinney & Snow (1985); MacWhinney (2000). For a discussion of how data of this sort can be used to investigate specific issues, see Stromswold (1996).

2. The great word hunt

1. Tomasello (2000b:406).
2. Garman (1979:183); Clark (1993:22).
3. Goldman (2001).
4. Clark (1993:22); Tamis-Lemonda et al. (1998:686).
5. Mervis & Bertrand (1995).
6. Goldfield & Reznick (1990); Rescorla, Mirak & Singh (2000).
7. P. Bloom (2002:35).
8. Clark (1993:13); P. Bloom (2002:43 & 49) offers somewhat more conservative estimates.
9. Clark (1993:13); Bloom & Markson (1998:68) place the estimate for six-year-olds at 10,000 words, as does Anglin (1993:118).
10. Anglin (1993:131).
11. Pinker (1994:150).
12. Ratner (1996:142); Morgan, Shi & Allopenna (1996:277).
13. R. Clark (1974:4).
14. Brown (1973:392–93).
15. Peters (1977).
16. Saffran, Aslin & Newport (1996).
17. Peters & Strömqvist (1996:215).

18. Jusczyk, Cutler & Redanz (1993).
19. Jusczyk, Houston & Newsome (1999); Newsome & Jusczyk (1995).
20. Mattys et al. (1999).
21. Shady & Gerken (1999).
22. Fernald & Mazzie (1991).
23. Peters (1985:1041); Slobin (1985:1169).
24. Clark (1993:40–41).
25. Peters (1983); Venditti, Jun & Bechman (1996:289).
26. Pinker & Prince (1988:150).
27. Greene (1969).
28. Berko (1958).
29. The picture of the wugs is from Berko (1958:154).
30. Clark (1993:102).
31. Based on data for the verb *make* in Maratsos (2000:195).
32. Marcus et al. (1992).
33. Lachter & Bever (1988:219).
34. For a discussion of how this might happen, see Bybee & Slobin (1982), and Albright (2002).
35. Xu & Pinker (1995).
36. Marcus (1995).
37. Maratsos (2000).
38. Clark (1993:145).
39. These examples are from Clark (1993:117–18).
40. Clark (1993:101, 116–17, & 200). See also Clark (1987b).
41. Clark (1993:101, 116–17, & 200).
42. Clark (1993:120).
43. Clark (1993:147–49).
44. Clark (1993:147).
45. Clark & Hecht (1982).
46. Clark (1993:102).
47. Clark & Hecht (1982:11).
48. Anglin (1993:97).
49. Clark (1993:148–49).
50. Clark (1993:117).
51. Clark, Gelman & Lane (1985).
52. Clark (1993:116).
53. Clark, Hecht & Mulford (1986).
54. Clark, Hecht & Mulford (1986:21).
55. Clark, Hecht & Mulford (1986:16 & 18).
56. Vogel & Raimy (2002).
57. Gordon (1985).

3. What's the meaning of this?

1. See the discussion in the preceding chapter as well as Bloom & Markson (1998:2) and the references cited there.
2. Balaban & Waxman (1996); see also Xu (1998).
3. Gentner (1982:306).
4. Clark (1993:29).
5. Goldfield (2000).
6. Sandhofer, Smith & Luo (2000).
7. For a summary, see Bloom (2002:94–95).
8. Wolf & Gardner (1979).
9. Goldfield & Snow (1993:310–14).
10. Piaget (1972).
11. Clark (1993:36).
12. Rescorla (1980); Clark (1993:34).
13. Hoek, Ingram & Gibson (1986).
14. Clark (1973); Rescorla (1980:325).
15. For additional examples, see Clark (1993:45).
16. Clark (1973); Thomson & Chapman (1977).
17. Bloom (2002:165–66); see also Diesendruck, Markson & Bloom (2003).
18. Rescorla (1980:331–32).
19. Rescorla (1980:329); Clark (1993:35).
20. Clark (1993:92).
21. Thomson & Chapman (1977).
22. Hoek, Ingram & Gibson (1986) report that overextension errors in comprehension are more likely to involve the substitution of an earlier learned (more familiar) word for a more recently learned (less familiar) word. For example, in one study of a one-year-old child, *shoe* (learned at 14 months) was interpreted to mean *boot* (learned at 17 months), *cat* (learned at 16 months) was used to mean *dog* (learned at 19 months), and so on.
23. Naigles & Gelman (1998); the figure is based on Hirsh-Pasek & Golinkoff (1996: 60).
24. McDonough (2002).
25. Markson & P. Bloom (1997).
26. Heibeck & Markman (1987).
27. Markson & Bloom (1997). Findings like these date back to pioneering work by Susan Carey and E. Bartlett in the 1970s. See, for example, S. Carey (1977).
28. Beals (1997), from which the following two examples are also taken.
29. See, for example, Markman (1989:26). For an earlier statement, see Macnamara (1982).

30. Clark (1993:50).
31. Clark (1993:51).
32. Rosch et al. (1976). Markman (1989:226) cites Keil (in press) as evidence that children rely heavily on perceptual appearances.
33. Tomasello (2000c).
34. Katz, Baker & Macnamara (1974). See also Bloom & Markson (1998) and Gelman & Taylor (1984).
35. Bloom & Kelemen (1995); Bloom et al.(1995).
36. Dickinson (1988).
37. Dickinson (1988); Bloom (2002:200–201).
38. Markman (1989:230).
39. Markman (1989:195).
40. Clark (1987a:13).
41. Smith (1979).
42. Markman (1989:198), citing Markman & Wachtel (1988); see also Diesendruck & Shatz (1997).
43. Markman (1989:230–31).
44. Clark (1996:63).
45. Naigles & Hoff-Ginsberg (1998:116).
46. Clark (1996:67).
47. Clark (1996:68–69). See also Bloom, Lifter & Hafitz (1980) and Behrend, Harris & Cartwright (1995).
48. Wagner (2001). See also Bloom, Lifter & Hafitz (1980) and Ingham (1992).
49. Gleitman (1990); Naigles (1990).
50. Hill, Collis & Lewis (1997). Another verb that seems to be difficult for children is *promise* – see Astington (1988) and Maas & Abbeduto (1998).
51. Maas & Abbeduto (2001).
52. Gropen et al. (1991).
53. Pinker (1989:26); Bowerman (1982b:338).
54. Sandhofer, Smith & Luo (2000).
55. Waxman & Klibanoff (2000); see also Akhtar (2002).
56. Hall, Burns & Pawluski (2003).
57. Harris & Morris (1986). See also Maratsos (1973, 1974); Ravn & Gelman (1984); and Gathercole (1982).
58. Sharpe, Fonte & Christe (1998); Ebeling & Gelman (1994).
59. Soja (1994).
60. Rice (1980).
61. Bornstein (1985a); Heibeck & Markman (1987).
62. Bornstein (1985b).
63. Shatz et al. (1996).

64. Braisby & Dockrell (1999).
65. Braisby & Dockrell (1999).
66. Johnson (1977).
67. Rosch Heider (1971).
68. Wynn (1990, 1992).
69. For a review, see P. Bloom (2002:217ff.).
70. Pollman (2003:22).
71. Tomasello (1987).
72. Johnston & Slobin (1979).
73. Johnston & Slobin (1979).
74. Chiat (1982).
75. Dale & Crain-Thoreson (1993).
76. Dale & Crain-Thoreson (1993).
77. Dale & Crain-Thoreson (1993).
78. Oshima-Takane, Takane & Shultz (1999:546).
79. Loveland (1984:548).
80. A similar conclusion is drawn in a study by Ricard, Girouard & Décarie (1999).

4. Words all in a row

1. Marcus et al. (1999).
2. Santelmann & Jusczyk (1998).
3. Miller & Chapman (1981). Damon's profile is from Clark (1993:25).
4. Brown (1973:55).
5. Pinker (1994: 269–70).
6. Braine (1963:4–5).
7. Bickerton (1999).
8. Tomasello (2000a).
9. Tomasello (1992, 2000b); Tomasello & Olgluin (1993); Tomasello et al. (1997).
10. Pinker (1984:123).
11. Déprez & Pierce (1993:43).
12. Akhtar (1997).
13. Macrae (1979:64).
14. Valian (1991:72–73).
15. P. Bloom (1990: 500).
16. L. Bloom (1970); P. Bloom (1990); Valian (1989, 1991).
17. P. Bloom (1990).
18. Gerken & McIntosh (1993); Shady & Gerken (1999).
19. Shafer et al. (1998).
20. Shady, Gerken & Jusezyk (1995).

21. Brown (1973:274).
22. Li, Leonard & Swanson (1999).
23. For some interesting ideas along these lines, see Slobin (1997).
24. Déprez & Pierce (1993:26).
25. These examples are from Déprez & Pierce (1993:34).
26. Déprez & Pierce (1993:34–35).
27. Drozd (1995:591).
28. Radford (1990:175).
29. Radford (1990:175 & 190).
30. However, Rispoli (1994) reports that the pronouns *he* and *they* are sometimes misused in this way, at least by some children.
31. Rispoli (1998:541).
32. Schütze (1999:752–53).
33. Valian (1991:52).
34. These examples, taken from the speech of several different children, are from Budwig (1989b:272).
35. Budwig (1989b:276); Thornton (2002).
36. From Bloom, Merkin & Wootten (1982:1086).
37. Clark and Clark (1977:352).
38. Stromswold (1995).
39. Yoshinaga (1996).
40. Kuczaj (1976); Stromswold (1990).
41. Allen (1995).
42. Nakayama (1987).
43. Limber (1973:176).
44. Radford (1990:140).
45. The examples and generalization are from Bloom et al. (1980); see also Scott (1984).
46. This technique was used in an experiment on relative clauses in Korean that I did with Miseon Lee (who also did the artwork) and Miho Choo.
47. Crain, McKee & Emiliani (1990).

5. What sentences mean

1. Adapted from Greenfield & Smith (1976:70).
2. Greenfield et al. (1985).
3. Bates & MacWhinney (1979).
4. Ninio (1992).
5. Hirsh-Pasek & Golinkoff (1991).
6. This picture is from Hirsh-Pasek & Golinkoff (1991:303).
7. Brown (1973:174).
8. Hirsh-Pasek & Golinkoff (1996, ch. 5).

9. De Villiers & de Villiers (1973); Slobin & Bever (1982); Thal & Flores (2001).
10. Akhtar & Tomasello (1997).
11. Pinker (1989:315).
12. Budwig (1990c:1233–34).
13. These were compiled from various sources by Pinker, Lebeaux & Frost (1987:204–205).
14. Budwig (1990c).
15. For example, Turner & Rommetveit (1967) and Baldie (1976).
16. These pictures are from Brown (1973:159).
17. De Villiers & de Villiers (1973); Pinker, Lebeaux & Frost (1987).
18. Gordon & Chafetz (1990).
19. Bever (1970).
20. The idea goes back to Rosenbaum (1967).
21. Chomsky (1969).
22. Lust (1981).
23. Chien & Wexler (1990:262).
24. See O'Grady (1997:22ff.) for a review of several studies.
25. Bloom et al. (1994).
26. Peterson & Dodsworth (1991:411–12).
27. Peterson & Dodsworth (1991).
28. Peterson (1990:438).
29. Peterson (1990:440–41).
30. This picture is from Roeper & de Villiers (1991:241).
31. Roeper & de Villiers (1991); see also Crain et al. (1996), who show that children can correctly interpret quantifier patterns of various sorts, including this one.
32. This picture is from Philip (1991:359).
33. Philip (1991).
34. Philip (1991, 1996).
35. Crain et al. (1996).

6. Talking the talk

1. Based on Oller (1980).
2. Fernald & McRoberts (1996:383); Werker et al. (1996:428); Hirsh-Pasek, Tucker & Golinkof (1996:453).
3. Mehler et al. (1996:106).
4. DeCasper & Fifer (1980).
5. Mehler et al. (1996:106).
6. Mehler et al. (1996:105).
7. DeCasper & Spence (1986).

8. DeCasper et al. (1994).
9. Moffit (1971); Eimas (1975). As noted by Jusczyk and Dorrah (1987), it is unclear where children have segmented these syllables into their component sounds at this point.
10. Eimas (1996:26); Kelly (1996:253).
11. Werker et al. (1996:431).
12. Eimas (1996:31).
13. Kuhl & Miller (1975); Hauser, Chomsky & Fitch (2002); Lieberman (1984).
14. Stager & Werker (1997).
15. Barton (1976a,b), cited by Ingram (1989:347).
16. Eilers & Oller (1976), cited by Ingram (1989:354–55).
17. See the summary in Ingram (1989:345ff.).
18. See Smolensky (1996:721) and Gerken (2002) for references.
19. Berko & Brown (1960).
20. Other references describing the same phenomenon can be found in Clark (1993:86).
21. Macken & Barton (1980).
22. Dodd (1975), cited by Clark (1993: 86).
23. The examples that follow are from Read (1975:55ff.); see also Bissex (1980).
24. Dodd (1979).
25. Vifman (1996:110–11); the babbling with reduplicated syllables is often called "canonical" while the more word-like babbling is labeled "variegated."
26. Lenneberg (1967).
27. See references and the review in Ingram (1989:112).
28. Ingram (1989:98).
29. This was proposed by Roman Jakobson, among others; see Ingram (1989:98–99).
30. Locke (1983:9–11).
31. de Boysson-Bardies, Sagart & Durand (1984).
32. de Boysson-Bardies and Marilyn Vihman (1991). There is a similar correlation for stop sounds ("p," "b," "t," "d," "k," "g"), with Swedish and English infants and adults producing more than their Japanese and French counterparts. The same is true for nasals ("m," "n," "ng"), where Japanese and French infants and adults are more prolific than the English and Swedish subjects.
33. See Ingram (1989: 361ff.).
34. Echols (1996:158) mentions an experiment in which imitation was used to elicit target words.

35. Peters & Menn (1993:754).
36. Clark (1993:85).
37. Kehoe & Stoel-Gammon (2001:402).
38. Stoel-Gammon (1985).
39. Ingram (1989:349); Stoel-Gammon (1985).
40. Stoel-Gammon (1985); Kehoe & Stoel-Gammon (2001:424) report the frequent occurrence of "s" and "sh" as well.
41. Ingram (1989:365).
42. Leopold (1939:172).
43. Clark (1993:26) reports this for one of the children she studied.
44. Jusczyk, Smolensky & Allocco (2002).
45. *faff* is from Gleitman & Wanner (1982:18); *tass* is from Wilson & Peters (1988:262); *na* is from French (1989:81); *way* is from Ingram (1976:31).
46. Based on data from three children aged 17–23 months, Echols (1996:154) reports that only 6 percent of syllables with primary stress were deleted.
47. These examples are from Kehoe & Stoel-Gammon (1997:124).
48. These examples are from Klein (1981).
49. Kehoe & Stoel-Gammon (1997); over 50 percent of unstressed nonfinal syllables were omitted in the Echols corpus.
50. The first two examples are from Kehoe & Stoel-Gammon (1997:125) and the last two from my daughter.
51. The *animal*, *banana*, and *alligator* examples are from Kehoe & Stoel-Gammon (1997:123, 126, & 138); the *elephant* example is from Demuth (1996b:172).
52. Echols (1996:154) reports that in her corpus only 36 percent of the sounds in unstressed and nonfinal syllables were correctly produced, compared to 66 percent in other syllables.
53. This data is from Klein (1981). She reports that 86 percent of Joshua's words maintained the number of syllables found in the adult word. In contrast, another child of the same age did this for only 11 percent of her multi-syllable words.

7. How do they do it?

1. Hauser, Chomsky & Fitch (2002:1574).
2. Hauser, Chomsky & Fitch (2002:1575).
3. Lust, Flynn & Foley (1996).
4. Bloom, Hood & Lightbown (1974); see also Sokolov & Moreton (1994) and Heath (1983).

5. Brown & Hanlon (1970); see also Demetras, Post & Snow (1986).
6. Maratsos (1983:732).
7. From McNeill (1966:68).
8. From Jean Berko Gleason, cited by Cazden (1972:92).
9. From Braine (1971:161).
10. Moerk (1991).
11. Strapp (1999).
12. From Hirsh-Pasek, Treiman & Schneiderman (1984:86).
13. Post (1994:155).
14. Morgan, Bonamo & Travis (1995). See also Marcus (1993).
15. Saxton (1997).
16. Saxton et al. (1998).
17. Saxton (1998).
18. Newport, Gleitman & Gleitman (1977).
19. Lieven (1994:62).
20. Based on Owens (1984:224).
21. Mannle & Tomasello (1987); Barton & Tomasello (1994). In fact, children as young as two and three make adjustments when speaking to younger siblings, shortening their sentences and producing more repetitions (Dunn & Kendrick (1982).
22. Fernald (1992).
23. Heath (1983); Ochs (1985); Lieven (1994); Crago, Allen & Hough-Eyamie (1997:74–75).
24. Heath (1983:95).
25. Heath (1983:86).
26. Pinker (1994:40).
27. Heath (1983:84); for the sake of exposition, I've converted Annie Mae's Black English Vernacular into my variety of English.
28. This is sometimes called the Interpretability Requirement; see, for example, O'Grady (1997:260).
29. Pinker (1994:278).
30. Hart & Risley (1995), cited by Pullum & Scholz (2002:44–45), place the figure at between 2.5 million and 7.5 million.
31. Snow (1977:41).
32. Heath (1983:91).
33. Stromswold (2001).
34. Stromswold (2001).
35. Gopnik & Crago (1991).
36. *New York Times* (July 15, 2003).
37. Gopnik (1990); Ullman & Gopnik (1999).
38. Vargha-Khadem et al. (1995); see also Elman et al. (1996:373ff.).

39. See Pinker (1994); Crain & Thornton (1998); and Guasti (2002) for reasonably accessible introductions to this idea. Chomsky (1995) offers a series of very technical essays on his views on Universal Grammar.
40. The proposal outlined here is based on Pinker (1984).
41. Bates & MacWhinney (1988:147).
42. Markman & Wechtel (1988).
43. Bloom (2002:68).
44. Bloom (2002:69).
45. Bloom (2002:11).
46. Versions of this idea have been proposed by Slobin (1985:1199); Berwick (1985:37); Wexler & Manzini (1987); Pinker (1989:364 & 1994:282), and O'Grady (1997:326), among others.
47. Bowerman (1996) is among those who has suggested that repeated exposure to the adult use of a word allows children to eventually cut out incorrect uses of the word in their own speech.
48. Clark (1987a); Saxton (1997).
49. See, for instance, Pinker (1999:68–69).

Appendix 1

1. Demuth (1996a); see also Stromswold (1996).
2. Brown (1973:54).

References

Akhtar, Nameera. 1997. Characterizing English-speaking children's understanding of SVO word order. Paper presented at the Child Language Research Forum, Stanford University.

2002. Relevance and early word learning. *Journal of Child Language* 29, 677–86.

Akhtar, N. and M. Tomasello. 1997. Young children's productivity with word order and verb morphology. *Developmental Psychology* 33, 952–66.

Albright, Adam. 2002. Islands of reliability for regular morphology: Evidence from Italian. *Language* 78, 684–709.

Allen, Joe. 1995. "Tense" doubling in early grammars. *Proceedings of the 19th Annual Boston University Conference on Language Development*, 48–59.

Anglin, Jeremy. 1993. Vocabulary development: A morphological analysis. *Monographs of the Society for Research in Child Development*. Serial No. 238, Vol. 58, No. 10.

Astington, Janet. 1988. Children's understanding of the speech act of promising. *Journal of Child Language* 15, 157–73.

Balaban, M. and S. Waxman. 1996. Words may facilitate categorization in 9-month-old infants. *Journal of Experimental Child Psychology* 64, 3–26.

Baldie, Brian. 1976. The acquisition of the passive voice. *Journal of Child Language* 3, 331–48.

Barton, D. 1976a. The role of perception on the acquisition of phonology. Doctoral dissertation, University of London.

1976b. Phonemic discrimination and the knowledge of words in children under three years of age. *Papers and Reports on Child Language Development* 11, 61–68.

Barton, M. and M. Tomasello. 1994. The rest of the family: The role of fathers and siblings in early language development. In C. Gallaway and B. Richards (eds.), *Input and interaction in language acquisition*. New York: Cambridge University Press, 109–34.

Bates, Elizabeth and Brian MacWhinney. 1979. The functionalist approach to the acquisition of grammar. In E. Ochs and B. Schieffelin (eds.), *Developmental Pragmatics*. New York: Academic Press, 167–211.

Bates, Elizabeth and Brian MacWhinney. 1988. What is functionalism? *Papers and Reports on Child Language Development* 27, 137–53.

Beals, Diane. 1997. Sources of support for learning words in conversation: Evidence from mealtimes. *Journal of Child Language* 24, 673–94.

Behrend, D., L. Harris, and K. Cartwright. 1995. Morphological cues to verb meaning: Verb inflections and the initial mapping of verb meanings. *Journal of Child Language* 22, 89–106.

Berko, Jean. 1958. The child's learning of English morphology. *Word* 14, 150–77.

Berko, Jean and Roger Brown. 1960. Psycholinguistic research methods. In P. Mussen (ed.), *Handbook of research methods in child development*. New York: Wiley, 517–57.

Berwick, Robert. 1985. *The acquisition of syntactic knowledge*. Cambridge, MA: MIT Press.

Bever, Thomas. 1970. The cognitive basis for linguistic structures. In J. R. Hayes (ed.), *Cognition and the development of language*. New York: Wiley, 274–353.

Bickerton, Derek. 1999. Creole languages, the Language Bioprogram Hypothesis, and language acquisition. In W. Ritchie and T. Bhatia (eds.), *Handbook of child language acquisition*. San Diego: Academic, 195–220.

Bissex, Glenda. 1980. *GNYS AT WRK: A child learns to write and read*. Cambridge, MA: Harvard University Press.

Bloom, Lois. 1970. *Language development: Form and function in emerging grammars*. Cambridge, MA: MIT Press.

Bloom, Lois, K. Lifter, and J. Hafitz. 1980. Semantics of verbs and the development of verb inflection in child language. *Language* 56, 386–412.

Bloom, Lois, Lois Hood, and Patsy Lightbown. 1974. Imitation in language development: If, when, and why. *Cognitive Psychology* 6, 380–420.

Bloom, Lois, Margaret Lahey, Lois Hood, Karin Lifter, and Kathleen Fiess. 1980. Complex sentences: Acquisition of syntactic connectives and

the semantic relations they encode. *Journal of Child Language* 7,
235–61.

Bloom, Lois, Susan Merkin, and Janet Wootten. 1982. *Wh*-questions:
Linguistic factors that contribute to the sequence of acquisition. *Child
Development* 53, 1084–92.

Bloom, Paul. 1990. Subjectless sentences in child language. *Linguistic
Inquiry* 21, 491–504.

2002. *How children learn the meanings of words*. Cambridge, MA: MIT
Press.

Bloom, Paul, Andrew Barss, Janet Nicol, and Laura Conway. 1994.
Children's knowledge of binding and coreference: Evidence from
spontaneous speech. *Language* 70, 53–71.

Bloom, Paul and Deborah Kelemen. 1995. Syntactic cues in the
acquisition of collective nouns. *Cognition* 56, 1–30.

Bloom, Paul, Deborah Kelemen, Amy Fountain, and Ellen Courtney.
1995. The acquisition of collective nouns. *Proceedings of the Boston
University Conference on Child Language* 19, 107–17.

Bloom, Paul and Lori Markson. 1998. Capacities underlying word
learning. *Trends in Cognitive Sciences* 2, 67–73.

Bornstein, Marc. 1985a. Colour-name versus shape-name learning in
young children. *Journal of Child Language* 12, 387–93.

1985b. On the development of color naming in young children: Data
and theory. *Brain and Language* 6, 72–93.

Bowerman, Melissa. 1982. Reorganizational processsses in lexical and
syntactic development. In E. Wanner and L. Gleitman (eds.), *Language
acquisition: The state of the art*. Cambridge, UK: Cambridge University
Press, 319–46.

1996. Argument structure and learnability: Is a solution in sight?
Proceedings of the Berkeley Linguistic Society 22, 454–68.

Braine, Martin. 1963. The ontogeny of English phrase structure: The first
phase. *Language* 39, 1–13.

1971. The acquisition of language in infant and child. In C. E. Reed
(ed.), *The learning of language*. New York: Appleton-Century-Crofts,
7–95.

Braisby, Nick and Julie Dockrell. 1999. Why is color naming difficult?
Journal of Child Language 26, 23–47.

Brown, Roger. 1973. *A first language: The early stages*. Cambridge, MA:
Harvard University Press.

Brown, Roger and Camille Hanlon. 1970. Derivational complexity and
order of acquisition in child speech. In J. R. Hayes (ed.), *Cognition and
the development of language*. New York: Wiley, 11–53.

Budwig, Nancy. 1989. The linguistic marking of agentivity and control in child language. *Journal of Child Language* 16, 263–84.

1990. The linguistic marking of non-prototypical agency: An exploration into children's uses of passives. *Linguistics* 28(6), 1221–52.

Bybee, Joan and Dan Slobin. 1982. Rules and schemas in the development and use of the English past tense. *Language* 58, 265–89.

Carey, Susan. 1977. The child as a word learner. In M. Halle, J. Bresnan, and G. Miller (eds.), *Linguistic theory and psychological reality*. Cambridge, MA: MIT Press, 264–93.

Cazden, Courtney. 1972. *Child language and education*. New York: Holt, Rinehart & Winston.

Chiat, Shulamuth. 1982. If I were you and you were me: The analysis of pronouns in a pronoun-reversing child. *Journal of Child Language* 9, 359–79.

Chien, Yu-Chin and Kenneth Wexler. 1990. Children's knowledge of locality conditions in binding as evidence for the modularity of syntax and pragmatics. *Language Acquisition* 1, 225–95.

Chomsky, Carol. 1969. *The acquisition of syntax in children from 5 to 10*. Cambridge, MA: MIT Press.

Chomsky, Noam. 1995. *The minimalist program*. Cambridge, MA: MIT Press.

Clark, Eve. 1973. What's in a word? On the child's acquisition of semantics in his first language. In T. Moore (ed.), *Cognitive development and the acquisition of language*. New York: Academic, 65–110.

1987a. The Principle of Contrast: A constraint on language acquisition. In B. MacWhinney (ed.), *Mechanisms of language acquisition*. Hillsdale, NJ: Erlbaum, 1–34.

1987b. The young word maker: A case study of innovation in the child's lexicon. In E. Wanner and L. Gleitman (eds.), *Language acquisition: The state of the art*. Cambridge, UK: Cambridge University Press, 390–425.

1993. *The lexicon in acquisition*. New York: Cambridge University Press.

1996. Early verbs, event types, and inflections. In C. Johnson and J. Gilbert (eds.), *Children's language*, Vol. IX. Mahwah, NJ: Erlbaum, 61–73.

Clark, Eve, Susan Gelman, and Nancy Lane. 1985. Compound nouns and category structure in young children. *Child Development* 56, 84–94.

Clark, Eve and Barbara Hecht. 1982. Learning to coin agent and instrument nouns. *Cognition* 12, 1–24.

Clark, Eve, Barbara Hecht, and Randa Mulford. 1986. Acquiring complex compounds: Affixes and word order in English. *Linguistics* 24, 7–29.

Clark, Herbert and Eve Clark. 1977. *Psychology and language: An introduction to psycholinguistics.* New York: Harcourt Brace Jovanovich.

Clark, Ruth. 1974. Performing without competence. *Journal of Child Language* 1, 1–10.

Crago, Martha, Shanley Allen, and Wendy Hough-Eyamie. 1997. Exploring innateness through cultural and linguistic variation. In M. Gopnik (ed.), *The inheritance and innateness of grammars.* New York: Oxford University Press, 111–40.

Crain, S., C. McKee, and M. Emiliani. 1990. Visiting relatives in Italy. In J. de Villiers and L. Frazier (eds.), *Language processing and language acquisition.* Boston: Reidel, 335–56.

Crain, Stephen and Rosalind Thornton. 1998. *Investigations in Universal Grammar.* Cambridge, MA: MIT Press.

Crain, Stephen, Rosalind Thornton, Carole Boster, Laura Conway, Diane Lillo-Martin, and Elaine Woodams. 1996. Quantification without qualification. *Language Acquisition* 5, 83–153.

Dale, Philip and Catherine Crain-Thoreson. 1993. Pronoun reversals: Who, when, and why? *Journal of Child Language* 20, 573–89.

de Boysson-Bardies, Bénédicte and Marilyn Vihman. 1991. Adaptation to language: Evidence from babbling and first words in four languages. *Language* 67, 297–319.

de Boysson-Bardies, Bénédicte, Laurent Sagart, and Catherine Durand. 1984. Discernable differences in the babbling of infants according to target language. *Journal of Child Language* 11, 1–16.

de Villiers, Jill and Peter de Villiers. 1973. Development of the use of word order in comprehension. *Journal of Psycholinguistic Research* 2, 331–41.

DeCasper, A. J. and W. P. Fifer. 1980. On human bonding: Newborns prefer their mothers' voices. *Science* 208, 1174–76.

DeCasper, A. J. and M. J. Spence. 1986. Prenatal maternal speech influences newborns' perception of speech sounds. *Infant Behavior and Development* 9, 133–50.

DeCasper, Anthony, Jean-Pierre LeCanuet, Marie-Claire Busnel, Carolyn Granier-Deferre, and Roselyne Maugeais. 1994. Fetal reactions to recurrent maternal speech. *Infant Behaviour and Development* 17, 159–64.

Demetras, M. J., Kathryn Post, and Catherine Snow. 1986. Feedback to first language learners: The role of repetitions and clarification questions. *Journal of Child Language* 13, 275–92.

Demuth, Katherine. 1996a. Collecting spontaneous production data. In D. McDaniel, C. McKee, and H. Cairns (eds.), *Methods for assessing children's syntax*. Cambridge, MA: MIT Press, 3–22.

1996b. The prosodic structure of early words. In J. Morgan and K. Demuth (eds.), *Signal to syntax*. Mahwah, NJ: Erlbaum, 171–84.

Déprez, Viviane and Amy Pierce. 1993. Negation and functional projections in early grammar. *Linguistic Inquiry* 24, 25–67.

Dickinson, D. K. 1988. Learning names for materials: Factors limiting and constraining hypotheses about word meaning. *Cognitive Development* 3, 15–35.

Diesendruck, Gil, Lori Markson, and Paul Bloom. 2003. Children's reliance on creator's intent in extending names for artifacts. *Psychological Science* 14, 164–68.

Diesendruck, Gil and Marilyn Shatz. 1997. The effect of perceptual similarity and linguistic input on children's acquisition of object labels. *Journal of Child Language* 24, 695–717.

Dodd, Barbara. 1975. Children's understanding of their own phonological forms, *Quarterly Journal of Experimental Psychology* 27, 165–72.

1979. Lip reading in infants: Attention to speech presented in and out of synchrony. *Cognitive Psychology* 11, 17–27.

Drozd, Kenneth. 1995. Child English pre-sentential negation as metalinguistic exclamatory negation. *Journal of Child Language* 22, 583–610.

Dunn, Judy and Carol Kendrick. 1982. The speech of two- and three-year-olds to infant siblings: "Baby talk" and the context of communication. *Journal of Child Language* 9, 579–95.

Ebeling, K. and S. Gelman. 1994. Children's use of context in interpreting *big* and *little*. *Child Development* 65, 1178–92.

Echols, Catharine. 1996. A role for stress in early speech segmentation. In J. Morgan and K. Demuth (eds.), *Signal to syntax*. Mahwah, NJ: Erlbaum, 151–70.

Eilers, R. and D. K. Oller. 1976. The role of speech discrimination in developmental sound distributions. *Journal of Child Language* 3, 319–29.

Eimas, Peter. 1975. Speech perception in early infancy. In L. Cohen and P. Salapatek (eds.), *Infant perception: From sensation to cognition*. Vol. II: *Perception of space, speech, and sound*, 193–231. New York: Academic Press.

1996. The perception and representation of speech by infants. In J. Morgan and K. Demuth (eds.), *Signal to syntax*. Mahwah, NJ: Erlbaum, 25–39.

Elman, Jaffrey, Elizabeth Bates, Mark Johnson, Annette Karmiloff-Smith, Domenico Pavisi, and Kim Plunkett. 1977. *Rethinking innateness: A connectionist perspective on development*. Cambridge, MA: MIT Press.

Fernald, Ann. 1992. Human maternal vocalisations to infants as biologically relevant signals: An evolutionary perspective. In J. H. Barkow, L. Cosmides, and J. Tooby (eds.), *The adapted mind: Evolutionary psychology and the generation of culture*. Oxford: Oxford University Press, 391–428.

Fernald, Ann and Claudia Mazzie. 1991. Prosody and focus in speech to infants and adults. *Developmental Psychology* 27, 209–21.

Fernald, Ann and Gerald McRoberts. 1996. Prosodic bootstrapping: A critical analysis of the argument and the evidence. In J. Morgan and K. Demuth (eds.), *Signal to syntax*. Mahwah, NJ: Erlbaum, 365–88.

French, Ann. 1989. The systematic acquisition of word forms by a child during the first fifty-word stage. *Journal of Child Language* 16, 69–90.

Garman, Michael. 1979. Early grammatical development. In P. Fletcher and M. Garman (eds.), *Language acquisition: Studies in first language development*. New York: Cambridge University Press, 177–208.

Gathercole, V. 1982. Decrements in children's responses to "big" and "tall": A reconsideration of the potential cognitive and semantic causes. *Journal of Experimental Child Psychology* 34, 156–73.

Gelman, S. and M. Taylor. 1984. How two-year-old children interpret proper and common names for unfamiliar objects. *Child Development* 55, 1535–40.

Gentner, Dedre. 1982. Why nouns are learned before verbs: Linguistic relativity vs. natural partitioning. In S. Kuczaj (ed.), *Language development*. Vol. II: *Language, cognition and culture*. Hillsdale, NJ: Erlbaum, 301–34.

Gerken, LouAnn. 2002. Early sensitivity to linguistic form. *Annual Review of Language Acquisition* 2, 1–36.

Gerken, LouAnn. and B. J. McIntosh. 1993. The interplay of function morphemes and prosody in early language. *Developmental Psychology* 29, 448–57.

Gleitman, Lila. 1990. The structural sources of verb meanings. *Language Acquisition* 1, 3–55.

Gleitman, Lila and Eric Wanner. 1982. Language acquisition: The state of the state of the art. In E. Wanner and L. Gleitman (eds.), *Language acquisition: The state of the art*. New York: Cambridge University Press, 3–48.

Goldfield, Beverly. 2000. Nouns before verbs in comprehension versus production: The view from pragmatics. *Journal of Child Language* 7, 501–20.

Goldfield, Beverly and J. Steven Reznick. 1990. Early lexical acquisition: Rate, content, and the vocabulary spurt. *Journal of Child Language* 17, 171–84.

Goldfield, Beverly and Catherine Snow. 1993. Individual differences in language acquisition. In Jean Berko (ed.), *The development of language*. 3rd edn. New York: Macmillan, 299–324.

Goldman, Herbert. 2001. Parental reports of "MAMA" sounds in infants: An exploratory study. *Journal of Child Language* 28, 497–506.

Gopnik, Myrna. 1990. Feature-blind grammar and dysphasia. *Nature* 344, p. 715.

Gopnik, Myrna and Martha Crago. 1991. Familial aggregation of a developmental language disorder. *Cognition* 39, 1–50.

Gordon, Peter. 1985. Level ordering in lexical development. *Cognition* 21, 73–93.

Gordon, Peter and Jill Chafetz. 1990. Verb-based versus class-based accounts of actionality effects in children's comprehension of passives. *Cognition* 36, 227–54.

Greene, Amsel. 1969. *Pullet surprises*. Glenview, IL: Scott, Foresman & Co.

Greenfield, Patricia, Judy Reilly, Campbell Leaper, and Nancy Baker. 1985. The structural and functional status of single-word utterances and their relationship to early multi-word speech. In M. Barrett (ed.), *Children's single-word speech*. New York: Wiley, 233–67.

Greenfield, Patricia and Joshua Smith. 1976. *The structure of communication in early language development*. New York: Academic Press.

Gropen, Jess, Steven Pinker, Michelle Hollander, and Richard Goldberg. 1991. Syntax and semantics in the acquisition of locative verbs. *Journal of Child Language* 18, 115–51.

Guasti, Maria. 2002. *Language acquisition: The growth of grammar*. Cambridge, MA: MIT Press.

Hall, D. Geoffrey, Tracey Burns, and Jodi Pawluski. 2003. Input and word learning: Caregivers' sensitivity to lexical category distinctions. *Journal of Child Language* 30, 711–29.

Harris, P. and J. Morris. 1986. The early acquisition of spatial adjectives: A cross-linguistic study. *Journal of Child Language* 13, 335–52.

Hart, Betty and Todd Risley. 1995. *Meaningful differences in the everyday experience of young children*. Baltimore: Paul H. Brookes.

Hauser, Marc, Noam Chomsky, and W. Tecumseh Fitch. 2002. The faculty of language: What is it, who has it, and how did it evolve? *Science* 298, 1569–79.

Heath, Shirley Brice. 1983. *Ways with words: Language, life and work in communities and classrooms*. New York: Cambridge University Press.

Heibeck, T. and E. Markman. 1987. Word learning in children: An examination of fast mapping. *Child Development* 58, 1021–34.

Hill, R., G. Collis and V. Lewis. 1997. Young children's understanding of the cognitive verb *forget*. *Journal of Child Language* 24, 57–79.

Hirsh-Pasek, Kathryn and Roberta Golinkoff. 1991. Language comprehension: A new look at old themes. In N. Krasnegor, D. Rumbaugh, R. Schiefelbusch, and M. Studdert-Kennedy (eds.), *Biological and behavioral determinants of language development*. Hillsdale, NJ: Erlbaum, 301–20.

   1996. The origins of grammar: Evidence from early language comprehension. Cambridge, MA: MIT Press.

Hirsh-Pasek, Kathryn, Rebecca Treiman, and Maita Schneiderman. 1984. Brown & Hanlon revisited: Mothers' sensitivity to ungrammatical forms. *Journal of Child Language* 11, 81–89.

Hirsh-Pasek, Kathryn, Michael Tucker, and Roberta Golinkoff. 1996. Dynamic systems theory: Reinterpreting "prosodic bootstrapping" and its role in language acquisition. In J. Morgan and K. Demuth (eds.), *Signal to syntax*. Mahwah, NJ: Erlbaum, 449–66.

Hoek, D., D. Ingram and D. Gibson. 1986. Some possible causes of children's early word overextensions. *Journal of Child Language* 13, 477–94.

Ingham, Richard. 1992. The optional subject phenomenon in young children's English: A case study. *Journal of Child Language* 19, 133–51.

Ingram, David. 1976. *Phonological disability in children*. London: Edward Arnold.

   1989. *First language acquisition: Method, description and explanation*. New York: Cambridge University Press.

Johnson, E. G. 1977. The development of color knowledge in children. *Child Development* 48, 308–11.

Johnston, Judith and Dan Slobin. 1979. The development of locative expressions in English, Italian, Serbo-Croatian and Turkish. *Journal of Child Language* 6, 529–45.

Jusczyk, P., A. Cutler, and N. Redanz. 1993. Infants' preference for the predominant stress pattern of English words. *Child Development* 64, 675–87.

Jusczyk, Peter and Carolyn Derrah. 1987. Representation of speech sounds by young infants. *Developmental Psychology* 23, 648–54.

Jusczyk, Peter, Derek Houston, and Mary Newsome. 1999. The beginnings of word segmentation in English-learning infants. *Cognitive Psychology* 39, 159–207.

Jusczyk, Peter, Paul Smolensky, and Theresa Allocco. 2002. How English-learning infants respond to markedness and faithfulness constraints. *Language Acquisition* 10, 31–73.

Katz, N, E. Baker, and J. Macnamara 1974. What's in a name: A study of how children learn common and proper names. *Child Development* 45, 469–73.

Kehoe, Margaret and Carol Stoel-Gammon. 1997. The acquisition of prosodic structure: An investigation of current accounts of children's prosodic development. *Language* 73, 113–44.

2001. Development of syllable structure in English-speaking children with particular reference to rhymes. *Journal of Child Language* 28, 393–432.

Kelly, Michael. 1996. The role of phononogy in grammatical category assignments. In J. Morgan and K. Demuth (eds.), *Signal to syntax*. Mahwah, NJ: Erlbaum, 249–62.

Klein, Harriet. 1981. Early perceptual strategies for the replication of consonants from polysyllabic lexical models. *Journal of Speech and Hearing Research* 24, 535–51.

Kuczaj, Stan. 1976. Arguments against Hurford's "Aux Copying Rule." *Journal of Child Language* 3, 423–27.

Kuhl, Patricia and J. D. Miller. 1975. Speech perception by the chinchilla: Voiced–voiceless distinction in alveolar plosive consonants. *Science* 190, 69–72.

Lachter, Joel and Thomas Bever. 1988. The relation between linguistic structure and associative theories of language learning: A constructive critique of some connectionist learning models. *Cognition* 28, 195–247.

Lenneberg, Eric. 1967. *Biological foundations of language*. New York: Wiley.

Leopold, Werner. 1939. *Speech development of a bilingual child: A Linguist's record*. Vol. I. Chicago: Northwestern University Press.

Li, Hsieh, Laurence Leonard, and Lori Swanson. 1999. Some differences between English plural noun inflections and third singular verb inflections in the input: The contributions of frequency, sentence position and duration. *Journal of Child Language* 26, 531–43.

Lieberman, Philip. 1984. *The biology and evolution of language*. Cambridge, MA: Harvard University Press.

Lieven, Elena. 1994. Crosslinguistic and crosscultural aspects of language addressed to children. In C. Gallway and B. Richards (eds.), *Input and interaction in language acquisition*. New York: Cambridge University Press, 56–73.

Limber, John. 1973. The genesis of complex sentences. In. T. Moore (ed.), *Cognitive development and the acquisition of language*. New York: Academic Press, 169–85.

Locke, John. 1983. *Phonological acquisition and change*. New York: Academic Press.

Loveland, Katherine. 1984. Learning about points of view: Spatial perspective and the acquisition of "I/you." *Journal of Child Language* 11, 535–56.

Lust, Barbara. 1981. Constraint on anaphora in child language: A prediction for a universal. In S. Tavakolian (ed.), *Language acquisition and linguistic theory*. Cambridge, MA: MIT Press, 74–96.

Lust, Barbara, Suzanne Flynn, and Claire Foley. 1996. What children know about what they say: Elicited imitation as a research method. In D. McDaniel, C. McKee, and H. Cairns (eds.), *Methods for assessing children's syntax*. Cambridge, MA: MIT Press, 55–76.

Maas, Fay and Leonard Abbeduto. 1998. Young children's understanding of promising: Methodological considerations. *Journal of Child Language* 25, 203–14.

2001. Children's judgments about intentionally and unintentionally broken promises. *Journal of Child Language* 28, 517–29.

Macken, Marlys and David Barton. 1980. The acquisition of the voicing contrast in English: A study of voice onset time in word-initial stop consonants. *Journal of Child Language* 7, 41–74.

Macnamara, John. 1982. *Names for things: A study of human learning*. Cambridge, MA: MIT Press.

Macrae, Alison. 1979. Combining meanings in early language. In P. Fletcher and M. Garmon (eds.), *Language acquisition*. Cambridge, UK: Cambridge University Press, 161–76.

MacWhinney, Brian. 2000. *The CHILDES project: Tools for analyzing talk*. 3rd edn. Mahwah, NJ: Erlbaum.

MacWhinney, Brian and Catherine Snow. 1985. The Child Language Data Exchange System. *Journal of Child Language* 12, 271–95.

Mannle, S. and M. Tomasello. 1987. Fathers, siblings and the bridge hypothesis. In K. Nelson and A. van Kleeck (eds.), *Children's language*. Vol. VI. Hillsdale, NJ: Erlbaum, 23–41.

Maratsos, Michael. 1973. Decrease in the understanding of the word "big" in preschool children. *Child Development* 44, 747–52.

1974. When is a high thing the big one? *Developmental Psychology* 10, 367–75.

1983. Some current issues in the study of the acquisition of grammar. In P. Mussen (ed.), *Handbook of child psychology*. Vol. III: *Cognitive development*. New York: John Wiley, 707–86.

2000. More overregularizations after all: New data and discussion on Marcus, Pinker, Ullman, Hollander, Rosen, and Xu. *Journal of Child Language* 27, 183–212.

Marcus, Gary. 1993. Negative evidence in language acquisition. *Cognition* 46, 53–85.

1995. Children's overgeneralizations of English plurals: A quantitative analysis. *Journal of Child Language* 22, 447–59.

Marcus, Gary, Michael Ullman, Steven Pinker, Michelle Hollander, T. John Rosen, and Fei Xu. 1992. *Overregularization in language acquisition*. Monographs of the Society for Research in Child Development 57 (serial no. 228).

Marcus, Gary, S. Vijayan, S. Bandi Rao, and P. Vishton. 1999. Rule learning by seven-month-old infants. *Science* 283 (1 January 1999), 77–80.

Markman, Ellen. 1989. *Categorization and naming in children: Problems of induction*. Cambridge, MA: MIT Press.

Markman, Ellen and G. F. Wachtel. 1988. Children's use of mutual exclusivity to constrain the meanings of words. *Cognitive Psychology* 20, 121–57.

Markson, Lori and Paul Bloom. 1997. Evidence against a dedicated system for word learning in children. *Nature* 385, 813–15.

Mattys, Sven, Peter Jusczyk, Paul Luce, and James Morgan. 1999. Word segmentation in infants: How phonotactics and prosody combine. *Cognitive Psychology* 38, 465–94.

McDonough, Laraine. 2002. Basic-level nouns: First learned but misunderstood. *Journal of Child Language* 29, 357–77.

McNeill, David. 1966. Developmental psycholinguistics. In F. Smith and G. Miller (eds.), *The genesis of language: A psycholinguistic approach*. Cambridge, MA: MIT Press, 15–84.

Mehler, Jacques, Emmanuel Dupoux, Thierry Nazzi, and Ghislaine Dehaene-Lambertz. 1996. Coping with linguistic diversity: The infant's viewpoint. In J. Morgan and K. Demuth (eds.), *Signal to syntax*. Mahwah, NJ: Erlbaum, 101–16.

Mervis, Carolyn and Jacquelyn Bertrand. 1995. Early lexical acquisition and the vocabulary spurt: A response to Goldfield & Reznick. *Journal of Child Language* 22, 461–68.

Miller, Jon and Robin Chapman. 1981. The relation between age and mean length of utterance in morphemes. *Journal of Speech and Hearing Research* 24, 154–61.

Moerk, Ernst. 1991. Positive evidence for negative evidence. *First Language* 11, 219–51.

Moffit, A. 1971. Consonant cue perception by twenty- to twenty-four-week-old infants. *Child Development* 42, 717–31.

Morgan, James, Katherine Bonamo, and Lisa Travis. 1995. Negative evidence on negative evidence. *Developmental Psychology* 31, 180–97.

Morgan, James, Rushen Shi, and Paul Allopenna. 1996. Perceptual bases of rudimentary grammatical categories: Toward a broader conceptualization of bootstrapping. In J. Morgan and K. Demuth (eds.), *Signal to syntax*. Mahwah, NJ: Erlbaum, 263–83.

Naigles, Letitia. 1990. Children use syntax to learn verb meanings. *Journal of Child Language* 17, 357–74.

Naigles, Letitia and Susan Gelman. 1995. Overextensions in comprehension and production revisited: Preferential-looking in a study of *dog, cat* and *cow. Journal of Child Language* 22, 19–46.

Naigles, Letitia and Erika Hoff-Ginsberg. 1998. Why are some verbs learned before other verbs? Effects of input frequency and structure on children's early verb use. *Journal of Child Language* 25, 95–120.

Nakayama, Mineharu. 1987. Performance factors in subject–auxiliary inversion. *Journal of Child Language* 14, 113–26.

Newport, Elissa, Henry Gleitman, and Lila Gleitman. 1977. Mother, I'd rather do it myself: Some effects and non-effects of maternal speech style. In C. Snow and C. Ferguson (eds.), *Talking to children: Language input and acquisition*. Cambridge, UK: Cambridge University Press, 109–49.

Newsome, Mary and Peter Jusczyk. 1995. Do infants use stress as a cue in segmenting fluent speech? In D. MacLaughlin and S. McEwan (eds.), *Proceedings of the 19th Annual Boston University Conference on Language Development*. Vol. II. Somerville, MA: Cascadilla Press, 415–26.

New York Times. 2003. Early voices: The leap to language. July 15.

Ninio, Anat. 1992. The relation of children's single word utterances to single word utterances in the input. *Journal of Child Language* 19, 87–110.

O'Grady, William. 1997. *Syntactic development*. Chicago: University of Chicago Press.

Ochs. Elinor. 1985. Variation and error: A sociolinguistic approach to language acquisition in Samoa. In D. Slobin (ed.), *The crosslinguistic study of language acquistion*. Vol. I: *The data*. Hillsdale, NJ: Erlbaum, 783–838.

Oller, D. K. 1980. The emergence of the sounds of speech in infancy. In G. Yeni-Komshian, J. Kavanaugh, and C. Ferguson (eds.), *Child Phonology*. Vol. I. *Production*. New York: Academic Press, 93–102.

Oshima-Takane, Yuriko, Yoshio Takane and Thomas Shultz. 1999. The learning of first and second person pronouns in English: Network models and analysis. *Journal of Child Language* 26, 545–75.

Owens, Robert Jr. 1984. *Language development. An introduction*. Columbus, OH: Charles E. Merrill.

Peters, Ann. 1977. Language learning strategies. *Language* 53, 560–73.
    1983. *The units of language acquisition*. New York: Cambridge University Press.
    1985. Language segmentation: Operating principles for the perception and analysis of language. In D. Slobin (ed.), *The crosslinguistic study of language acquisition*. Vol. II: *Theoretical issues*. Hillsdale, NJ: Erlbaum, 1029–68.

Peters, Ann and Lise Menn. 1993. False starts and filler syllables: Ways to learn grammatical morphemes. *Language* 69, 742–77.

Peters, Ann and Sven Strömqvist. 1996. The role of prosody in the acquisition of grammatical morphemes. In J. Morgan and K. Demuth (eds.), *Signal to syntax*. Mahwah, NJ: Erlbaum, 215–32.

Peterson, Carole. 1990. The who, when and where of early narratives. *Journal of Child Language* 17, 433–55.

Peterson, Carole and Pamela Dodsworth. 1991. A longitudinal analysis of young children's cohesion and noun specification in narratives. *Journal of Child Language* 18, 397–415.

Philip, Bill. 1991. Spreading in the acquisition of universal quantifiers. *Proceedings of the Tenth West Coast Conference on Formal Linguistics*. Stanford, CSLI, 359–73.
    1996. The event quantificational account of symmetrical interpretation and a denial of implausible infelicity. *Boston University Conference on Language Development* 20, 564–75.

Piaget, Jean. 1972. *The child's conception of the world*. Totawa, NJ: Littlefield, Adams & Co.

Pinker, Steven. 1984. *Language learnability and language development*. Cambridge, MA: Harvard University Press.
    1989. *Learnability and cognition*. Cambridge, MA: MIT Press.
    1994. *The language instinct*. New York: Morrow & Co.
    1999. *Words and rules*. New York: Basic Books.

Pinker, Steven, David Lebeaux, and Loren Frost. 1987. Productivity and constraints in the acquisition of the passive. *Cognition* 26, 195–267.

Pinker, Steven and Alan Prince. 1988. On language and connectionism: Analysis of a Parallel Distributed Processing model of language acquisition. *Cognition* 28, 73–193.

Pollman, Thijs. 2003. Some principles involved in the acquisition of number words. *Language Acquisition* 11, 1–13.

Post, Kathryn. 1994. Negative evidence in the language learning environment of later-borns in a rural Florida community. In J. Sokolov and C. Snow (eds.), *Handbook of research in language development using CHILDES*. Hillsdale, NJ: Erlbaum, 132–73.

Pullum, Geoffrey and Barbara Scholz. 2002. Empirical assessment of stimulus poverty arguments. *Linguistic Review* 19, 9–50.

Radford, Andrew. 1990. *Syntactic theory and the acquisition of English syntax*. Cambridge, MA: Blackwell.

Ratner, Nan. 1996. From "signal to syntax": But what is the nature of the signal? In J. Morgan and K. Demuth (eds.), *Signal to syntax*. Mahwah, NJ: Erlbaum, 135–50.

Ravn, Karen and Susan Gelman. 1984. Rule usage in children's understanding of "big" and "little." *Child Development* 55, 2141–50.

Read, Charles. 1975. Children's categorization of speech sounds in English. (Research Report No. 17). Urbana, IL: National Council of Teachers of English.

Rescorla, Leslie. 1980. Overextension in early language development. *Journal of Child Language* 7, 321–35.

Rescorla, Leslie, Jennifer Mirak, and Leher Singh. 2000. Vocabulary growth in late talkers: Lexical development from 2;0 to 3;0. *Journal of Child Language* 27, 293–311.

Ricard, Marcelle, Pascale Girouard, and Thérèse Gouin Décarie. 1999. Personal pronouns and perspective taking in toddlers. *Journal of Child Language* 26, 681–97.

Rice, Mabel. 1980. *Cognition to language: Categories, word meanings, and training*. Baltimore: University Park Press.

Rispoli, Matthew. 1994. Pronoun case overextensions and paradigm building. *Journal of Child Language* 21, 157–72.

1998. Patterns of pronoun case error. *Journal of Child Language* 25, 533–54.

Roeper, Thomas and Jill de Villiers. 1991. The emergence of bound variable structures. In T. Maxfield and B. Plunkett (eds.), *Papers on the acquisition of WH. University of Massachusetts Occasional Papers.* Amherst, MA: GLSA Publications, 225–65.

Rosch Heider, Eleanor. 1971. "Focal" color areas and the development of color names. *Developmental Psychology* 4, 447–55.

Rosch, Eleanor, Carolyn Mervis, Wayne Gray, David Johnson, and Penny Boyes-Braem. 1976. Basic objects in natural categories. *Cognitive Psychology* 8, 382–439.

Rosenbaum, Peter. 1967. *The grammar of English predicate complement constructions.* Cambridge, MA: MIT Press.

Saffran, Jenny, Richard Aslin, and Elissa Newport. 1996. Statistical learning by eight-month-old infants. *Science* 274, 1926–28.

Sandhofer, Catherine, Linda Smith and Jun Luo. 2000. Counting nouns and verbs in the input: Differential frequencies, different kinds of learning. *Journal of Child Language* 7, 561–85.

Santelmann, Lynn and Peter Jusczyk. 1998. Sensitivity to discontinuous dependencies in language learners: Evidence for limitations in processing space. *Cognition* 69, 105–34.

Saxton, Matthew. 1997. The Contrast Theory of negative evidence. *Journal of Child Language* 24, 139–61.

1998. Negative evidence and negative feedback: Immediate effects on the grammaticality of child speech. Unpublished ms., Royal Holloway, University of London.

Saxton, Matthew, Bela Kulscar, Greer Marshall, and Mandeep Rupra. 1998. Longer-term effects of corrective input: An experimental approach. *Journal of Child Language* 25, 701–21.

Schütze, Carson. 1999. Different rates of pronoun case errors: Comments on Rispoli (1998). *Journal of Child Language* 28, 749–55.

Scott, Cheryl. 1984. Adverbial connectivity in conversations of children 6 to 12. *Journal of Child Language* 11, 423–52.

Shady, Michele and LouAnn Gerken. 1999. Grammatical and caregiver cues in early sentence comprehension. *Journal of Child Language* 26, 163–75.

Shady, Michele, LouAnn Gerken, and Peter Jusczyk. 1995. Some evidence of sensitivity to prosody and word order in ten-month-olds. *Proceedings of the 19th Annual Boston University Conference on Language Development*, 553–62.

Shafer, Valerie, David Shucard, Janet Shucard, and LouAnn Gerken. 1998. An electrophysiological study of infants' sensitivity to English function morphemes. *Journal of Speech, Language and Hearing Research* 41, 874–86.

Sharpe, Dean, Isabel Fonte, and Elisabeth Christe. 1998. Big mice, big animals, big problems: The acquisition of adjective interpretation rules. *Proceedings of the 22nd Boston University Conference on Language Development*, 675–83.

Shatz, Marilyn, Douglas Behrend, Susan Gelman, and Karen Ebeling. 1996. Colour term knowledge in two-year-olds: Evidence for early competence. *Journal of Child Language* 23, 177–99.

Slobin, Dan. 1985. Crosslinguistic evidence for the language-making capacity. In D. Slobin (ed.), *The crosslinguistic study of language acquisition*. Vol. II: *Theoretical issues*. Hillsdale, NJ: Erlbaum, 1157–1256.

    1997. The origins of grammaticizable notions: Beyond the individual mind. In D. Slobin (ed.), *The crosslinguistic study of language acquisition*. Vol. V: *Expanding the contexts*. Hillsdale, NJ: Erlbaum, 265–323.

Slobin, Dan and Thomas Bever. 1982. Children use canonical sentence schemas: A crosslinguistic study of word order and inflections. *Cognition* 12, 229–65.

Smith, C. L. 1979. Children's understanding of natural language hierarchies. *Journal of Experimental Child Psychology* 27, 437–58.

Smolensky, Paul. 1996. On the comprehension/production dilemma in child language. *Linguistic Inquiry* 27, 720–31.

Snow, Catherine. 1977. Mothers' speech research: From input to interaction. In C. Snow and C. Ferguson (eds.), *Talking to children: Language input and acquisition*. London: Cambridge University Press, 31–49.

Soja, Nancy. 1994. Young children's concept of color and its relation to the acquisition of color words. *Child Development* 65, 918–37.

Sokolov, Jeffrey and Joy Moreton. 1994. Individual differences in linguistic imitativeness. In J. Sokolov and C. Snow (eds.), *Handbook of research in language development using CHILDES*. Hillsdale, NJ: Erlbaum, 174–209.

Stager, Christine and Janet Werker. 1997. Infants listen for more phonetic detail in speech perception than in word-learning tasks. *Nature* 388, 381–82.

Stoel-Gammon, Carol. 1985. Phonetic inventories, 15–24 months. *Journal of Speech and Hearing Research* 28, 505–12.

Strapp, Chehalis. 1999. Mothers', fathers', and siblings' responses to children's language errors: Comparing sources of negative evidence. *Journal of Child Language* 26, 373–91.

Stromswold, Karin. 1990. Learnability and the acquisition of auxiliaries. Ph.D. dissertation. MIT.

1995. The acquisition of subject and object *wh*-questions. *Language Acquisition* 4, 5–48.

1996. Analyzing children's spontaneous speech. In D. McDaniel, C. McKee, and H. Cairns (eds.), *Methods for assessing children's syntax*. Cambridge, MA: MIT Press, 23–53.

Stromswold, Karin. 2001. The heritability of language: A review and metaanalysis of twin, adoption and linkage studies. *Language* 77, 647–723.

Tamis-Lemonda, Catherine, Marc Bornstein, Ronit Kahana-Kalman, Lisa Baumwell, and Lisa Cyphers. 1998. Predicting variation in the timing of language milestones in the second year: An events history approach. *Journal of Child Language* 25, 675–700.

Thal, Donna and Melanie Flores. 2001. Development of sentence interpretation strategies by typically developing and late-talking toddlers. *Journal of Child Language* 28, 173–93.

Thomson, J. and R. Chapman. 1977. Who is "Daddy" revisited: The status of two-year-olds' over-extended words in use and comprehension. *Journal of Child Language* 4, 359–75.

Thornton, Rosalind. 2002. Let's change the subject: Focus movement in early grammar. *Language Acquisition* 10, 229–71.

Tomasello, Michael. 1987. Learning to use prepositions: A case study. *Journal of Child Language* 14, 79–98.

1992. *First verbs: A case study of early grammatical development*. New York: Cambridge University Press.

2000a. A usage-based approach to child language acquisition. *Berkeley Linguistic Society* 26, 305–19.

2000b. The item-based nature of children's early syntactic development. *Trends in Cognitive Sciences* 4, 156–63.

2000c. The social-pragmatic theory of word learning. *Pragmatics* 10, 401–13.

Tomasello, Michael, N. Akhtar, K. Dodson, and L. Rekau. 1997. Differential productivity in young children's use of nouns and verbs. *Journal of Child Language* 24, 373–87.

Tomasello, Michael and R. Olgluin. 1993. Twenty-three-month-old children have a grammatical category of noun. *Cognitive Development* 8, 451–64.

Turner, Elizabeth Ann and Ragnar Rommetveit. 1967. The acquisition of sentence voice and reversibility. *Child Development* 38, 649–60.

Ullman, Michael and Myrna Gopnik. 1999. Inflectional morphology in a family with inherited specific language impairment. *Applied Psycholinguistics* 20, 51–117.

Valian, Virginia. 1989. Children's production of subjects: Competence, performance and the null subject parameter. *Papers and Reports on Child Language Development* 28, 156–63.

1991. Syntactic subjects in the early speech of American and Italian children. *Cognition* 40, 21–81.

Vargha-Khadem, Faraneh, Kate Watkins, Katie Alcock, Paul Fletcher, and Richard Passingham. 1995. Praxis and non-verbal cognitive deficits in a large family with a genetically transmitted speech and language disorder. *Proceedings of the National Academy of Sciences of the United States of America* 92, 930–33.

Venditti, Jennifer, Sun-Ah Jun, and Mary Bechman. 1996. Prosodic cues to syntactic and other linguistic structures in Japanese, Korean, and English. In J. Morgan and K. Demuth (eds.), *Signal to syntax*. Mahwah, NJ: Erlbaum, 287–311.

Vifman, Marilyn. 1996. *Phonological development: The origins of language in the child*. Cambridge, MA: Blackwell.

Vogel, Irene and Eric Raimy. 2002. The acquisition of compound vs. phrasal stress: The role of prosodic constituents. *Journal of Child Language* 29, 225–50.

Wagner, Laura. 2001. Aspectual influences on early tense comprehension. *Journal of Child Language* 28, 661–81.

Waxman, S. R. and R. Klibanoff. 2000. The role of comparison in the acquisition of novel adjectives. *Developmental Psychology* 36, 571–81.

Werker, Janet, Valerie Lloyd, Judith Pegg and Linda Polka. 1996. Putting the baby in the bootstraps: Toward a more complete understanding of the role of the input in infant speech processing. In J. Morgan and K. Demuth (eds.), *Signal to syntax*. Mahwah, NJ: Erlbaum, 427–47.

Wexler, Kenneth and M. Rita Manzini. 1987. Parameters and learnability in binding theory. In T. Roeper and E. Williams (eds.), *Parameter setting*. Dordrecht: Reidel, 41–76.

Wilson, Bob and Ann Peters. 1988. What are you cookin' on a hot? *Language* 64, 249–73.

Wolf, Dennie and Howard Gardner. 1979. Style and sequence in symbolic play. In M. Franklin and N. Smith (eds.), *Symbolic functioning in childhood*. Hillsdale, NJ: Erlbaum, 117–38.

Wynn, Karen. 1990. Children's understanding of counting. *Cognition* 36, 155–93.

1992. Children's acquisition of number words and the counting system. *Cognitive Psychology* 24, 220–51.

Xu, Fei. 1998. Distinct labels provide pointers to distinct sortals for 9-month-old infants. *Proceedings of the 22nd Boston University Conference on Language Development*, 791–96.

Xu, Fei and Steven Pinker. 1995. Weird past tense forms. *Journal of Child Language* 22, 531–56.

Yoshinaga, Naoko. 1996. *Wh*-questions: A comparative study of their form and acquisition in Japanese. Ph.D. dissertation, University of Hawaii.

Index